D0204308

THE FAST TRACK GUIDE TO

SPEAKING IN PUBLIC

SELECTED OTHER BOOKS BY DR. JAN YAGER

NONFICTION

Work Less, Do More: The 14-Day Productivity Makeover (2nd edition)

Productive Relationships

Grow Global

When Friendship Hurts

Friendshifts: The Power of Friendship and How It Shapes Our Lives

Effective Business and Nonfiction Writing

Road Signs on Life's Journey

365 Daily Affirmations for Happiness

365 Daily Affirmations for Time Management

365 Daily Affirmations for Creative Weight Management

365 Daily Affirmations for Friendship

Business Protocol: How to Survive & Succeed in Business

Who's That Sitting at My Desk?: Workship, Friendship, or Foe?

125 Ways to Meet the Love of Your Life

Creative Time Management for the New Millennium

Career Opportunities in the Film Industry (with Fred Yager)

Career Opportunities in the Publishing Industry (with Fred Yager)

FICTION

The Pretty One

Untimely Death (with Fred Yager)

Just Your Everyday People (with Fred Yager)

The Cantaloupe Cat (illustrated by Mitzi Lyman)

THE FAST TRACK GUIDE TO

SPEAKING ᴵᴺ PUBLIC

JAN YAGER, Pʜ.D.

Hᴀɴɴᴀᴄʀᴏɪx Cʀᴇᴇᴋ Bᴏᴏᴋs, Iɴᴄ.
Stamford, Connecticut

Published by:
Hannacroix Creek Books, Inc.
1127 High Ridge Road, #110
Stamford, CT 06905 USA
http://www.hannacroixcreekbooks.com
hannacroix@aol.com

ISBN: 978-1-889262-65-9 (hardcover)
ISBN: 978-1-889262-68-0 (trade paperback)

Library of Congress Cataloging-in-Publication Data

Yager, Jan, 1948-
The fast track guide to speaking in public / Jan Yager.
p. cm.
ISBN 978-1-889262-65-9 (hardcover) -- ISBN 978-1-889262-68-0 (trade pbk.)
1. Public speaking. I. Title.
PN4129.15.Y344 2013
808.5'1--dc23
   2012026943

CONTENTS

Chapter 1
GETTING STARTED AS A SPEAKER

When I spoke in Kolkata, India before approximately two-hundred fifty mutual fund managers, I knew that I was connecting with the audience without even having to review the video clip that the meeting planner posted at www.youtube.com because I could sense it in the room. Although I couldn't see many faces because of the lighting and the way the podium was set up, I could see at least a few people right in the front and it was their connection to my words that kept me going.

That speaking engagement is a wonderful example of why I speak. Not only did I have the opportunity to share my expertise and insights about work relationships, time management, and achieving greater productivity and work-life balance, but I also got to travel to an amazing part of the world. I met extraordinary men and women, and even children and teens since the meeting planner asked me to also speak at a Rotary Club in Kolkata where there were many children and teens performing and in the audience.

Everyone knows that today you need excellent communication and computer skills to get ahead in business. Being well versed in business protocol will certainly help as well. But you can add to that list another basic competence that can make or break your career: your presentation skills. Being able to research, write, and deliver a memorable and effective speech, whether it's a ten-minute presentation on a panel or a forty-five minute keynote address at an international conference, is a skill that should accelerate your professional, and even your personal, success.

The exciting part about speaking in public, once you learn to embrace the unpredictable nature of the experience, rather than fear it, is that you do have to "think on your feet" and to learn to be flexible. You might use the same opening story before several different audiences and it works again and again, but you get the instinct, this time, just as you're about to speak that there's something going on with the particular audience in this room that tells you, that cries out to you, "Use a different story."

And you follow your instinct and you find out later that it was the right decision because there was something in that "signature" story that would have offended the majority of people in that specific group.

You *can* master public speaking! This book will help you with that goal by providing information as well as true-life anecdotes and examples from my own professional and personal experiences, the research I've done, as well as interviews I've conducted or communications I've received just for this book with outstanding speakers from around the world.

Every speaker, even those commanding six figures for just one speech, started where you are right now: at the beginning. And if you've been speaking, for work or professionally, and you think you could use a refresher course, or just some input from someone new, this book may just be what you're looking for as well.

In his *New York Times* article, "Social Anxiety: New Focus Leads to Insights and Therapy," psychologist and journalist Daniel Goleman noted that "the most frequent fear in one survey of 3,000 adults was found to be speaking before a group."[1]

There's also an old cliché that public speaking is feared more than death. I don't know where that notion came from or what study it is based upon, but I do know that, while none of us can do anything about death, we can all do something about how comfortable we are speaking in public.

---

[1] You will find the complete citation for this reference in the References section in the back of this book.

Are you afraid to speak in public?

If you are asked to make a speech, do you find yourself getting butterflies in your stomach from the moment you accept an invitation to speak until you give your address months, weeks, days, or even hours later?

If you are not fearful of speaking in public, do you still feel that your speaking skills could use some improvement based on feedback you've received or your own self-assessment?

You *can* get over your fear of speaking and improve your speaking skills.

Fortunately the basic techniques that you need to be a skilled speaker can be taught; becoming more secure in your speaking ability should help to decrease your fear of speaking. You will learn essential public speaking techniques in this book. Despite what you may have thought till now, being a dynamic speaker is rarely something that happens at birth. Yes, some may be more comfortable in front of an audience than others. But you can learn how to welcome, and not dread, getting in front of an audience and speaking in public. The tools that professional speakers use to craft and deliver a memorable speech are there for you to learn and use.

Few professionals "wing it," even if you think, sitting in that audience and listening to their speech, that that's what they're doing. They've planned, practiced, and prepped for that presentation, whether it's five minutes, half an hour, or an all-day seminar. It took hard work to make that speech look as if it were extemporaneous and unplanned! Some speakers have been working on their craft for years, even decades. In this book, you'll discover the secrets of professional speakers; if you apply these secrets, you will be on the path to becoming a more confident speaker in your own right with the pride of knowing that your speech made a difference in the lives of those in your audience. It is with that goal in mind that I pledged to research, write, and publish this book.

It is called *The Fast Track Guide to Speaking in Public* because the goal of this book is to help the novice speaker to fast track his or her career. You can do that by avoiding as many of the pitfalls of public speaking as possible by being as prepared as you can be through research, related to a specific topic that you are speaking on as well as on speaking in general, such as through reading this book or attending a speaking workshop or working with a coach, and by the practice that is advocated in these pages.

For the more experienced speaker, this book provides a useful review of your craft as well as exposure to the speaking techniques and experiences of others from whom you may learn as you improve your own content and style of each speech that you deliver.

The founder of the National Speakers Association, Cavett Roberts, espoused the belief that working hard at the craft of speaking would help a speaker's presentation skills. *The Fast Track Guide to Speaking in Public* will hopefully make that hard work more fun and pleasant because you'll be guided by a seasoned pro along the way. Everything I'll be teaching you I've learned through four decades of speaking throughout the U.S. and internationally as well as training in public speaking going as far back as a course I took in public speaking as a college senior.

In this guide on how to prepare, and deliver, various types of speeches, you will discover basic steps that apply when you are a presenter, whatever the length of your program. You will also be reminded that you will want to develop your own speaking style; and, as you learn some of the proven techniques for overcoming stage fright or speaker fear, you will be able to apply those suggestions to your own situations.

I will also share with you some innovative ideas for how to get extra mileage out of your speech by recording it, rewriting it as an article for your company newsletter, adapting it as the basis of a blog, or even expanding it to become a book, and even using it as the core of an e-learning training program that you decide to develop. For example, the book you are now reading actually had its origins as a workshop on public speaking that I conducted in 2005. And now, seven years later, after adding new research and professional experiences, the 15,000 words that I wrote out as the foundation and basics of that workshop I have expanded into a 56,600 word book.

In this book, you'll also learn how to get beyond "just getting through" whatever speech you've been asked to give, as if it's medicine you've been instructed to take. Instead, you will be mastering how to do your presentation well, and hopefully learning how to even enjoy speaking in public, whether you want to keep speaking and become a professional speaker or if you just want to be able to speak effectively and without dread whenever you're asked to do it.

I like to define myself as a writer who speaks rather than a speaker who writes. As hard as writing might be, I definitely find public speaking to be even more challenging. Writing allows me to compose, and rewrite; until I am pleased with my words, I can rewrite something in the privacy of my office, at the local coffee shop, or on a train or airplane on my laptop. I can rewrite something once, twice, or even twenty or more times. I don't have to share those words with anyone till I'm absolutely comfortable with my words. Then, if I choose to, I can publish those words and I can let those words remain permanent.

But when I speak, there is this amazing x-factor known as the audience. Even if I've prepared a written speech, and rehearsed and practiced it a dozen times, there is a dynamic that is called into play that makes the speaking experience both exhilarating and unique — but also somewhat unpredictable and intimidating. What if the audience doesn't "like" me or like what I have to say?

What you will learn in this book is that the most important person to please when you speak is yourself. Like yourself. Feel confident in the ideas that you have to share, feel empowered by the research you've compiled, the writing you've done on the topic, whether it's an outline, a fully written out speech, or keywords jotted down on your smart phone or on an index card, and you'll be amazed at the results that you will get.

Be open to feedback, so you can improve, without feeling like you're being criticized. By that I mean both the formal feedback from evaluations at the end of your speech from the audience's body language that you are observing while you're speaking, and from the e-mails or other written communications you received days, months, or years after your speech about the impact your words made on someone's life.

Reading *The Fast Track Guide to Speaking in Public* will help you to see more clearly why some speeches are dynamic, memorable, and helpful to an audience, and a speaker gets thunderous applause, and someone's reputation and career get pushed ahead while other speeches are boring, poorly received, and definitely don't advance anyone's career.

I have been speaking as far back as my earliest elementary school days. In high school, I still can see myself delivering a speech to my class of over 1,000 about why they should vote for me for school secretary. Then, in college, I took an excellent public speaking course; one of the speeches that I researched and delivered eventually became the subject matter for my first published nonfiction book. Years later, I taught a graduate course in communications; speakers are, essentially, communicators.

Because I am a book author, I am often asked to speak about one of my many published books. For some reason, there is an assumption that book authors should be able to speak in public, even though writing a book and giving a speech rely on very different skills (although the writing of a speech may be related to writing a book). But certainly the delivery of a speech is related more to acting and performance skills than to literary ones. Fortunately I studied acting in high school at the American Academy of Dramatic Arts in New York City and I even went to professional acting school, the Gene Frankel Theatre Workshop, during my college years. Those acting experiences have been useful to me over the years that I have been speaking.

Then, sixteen years ago, I decided to take my speaking career much more seriously. I joined the National Speakers Association. I threw myself into becoming a better speaking by getting to know, and observe, other speakers, and to gain a better understanding of the unique skills that you need if you are to be a memorable speaker, whether you give one speech or you make it part or all of your career.

Before my decision to become more serious about my speaking career, I basically delivered a speech if someone sought me out and asked me to do it, or if I taught a course because I had researched a subject and wanted to share my expertise. I had been teaching at the college level for decades, in both a full-time and adjunct or part-time capacity, but now I wanted to also speak before a variety of corporate, association, and government agencies. I still wanted to primarily be a writer, but now I wanted to be "a writer who speaks."

Speaking offers everyone, whether you are a writer, an executive at a company, or an entrepreneur, the opportunity to share your knowledge, to inspire, to motivate, and to change lives.

Communicating orally is definitely not the same as communicating in writing. The written word can be chiseled in stone, if you like, and never changed. Who reads the words may change, but the words themselves remain constant.

That is the exact opposite of a speech. Even if you write out your speech and learn it so well that you seem as if you are making it up as you go along, even though the speech is really very planned and rehearsed, unless you are doing a webinar and your audience is anonymous, your audience is right there in front of you. And oftentimes your audience becomes a part of your presentation; you draw upon their everyday experiences and their input. (There is a movement toward interactive books, with readers sharing their reactions to a passage or an entire book with the author, and trying to influence the literary work, that is still in the future.)

Audiences do impact on speakers; this book will show you how to become comfortable with that reality so that you are able to master public speaking.

So the first step in this process of learning how to speak more effectively in public is to ask, and answer, this very crucial question: Why do you want to speak in public?

You may have several answers to that question. Here are some of the most common reasons that may have led you to pick up this book:

1. Your boss asks you to make a presentation on behalf of your company at the upcoming annual association meeting.

2. You have been asked to appear on a panel of experts at an upcoming conference. This will be an honor for you and it might lead to new customers.

3. Your best friend is getting married and he wants you to give the toast at the wedding reception.

4. Your local community organization asks you to emcee their main fundraising event for the year, a talent show.

5. Your startup is at the point that you need extra funding; you have been asked to make a presentation before a group of investors, who will decide if they want to put capital into your project.

Do you have a reason that is missing from the list above? Write that reason or reasons down now.

These are just some of the myriad of reasons that learning how to be a better public speaker will mean a lot to you both professionally and personally.

Rather than finding some excuse for not speaking in public, take the time to master the skills of a public speaker so that you will shine on the platform. You might even find that you enjoy it so much that you want to make it a bigger part of your career, or even focus on speaking rather than your "day" job. That's what happened to Warren Greshes. I heard Warren, who now speaks full-time, present at the local chapter of the National Speakers Association in New York City and he is a memorable and excellent speaker. He shared with out group how his career as a professional speaker evolved. He told us that when he started speaking professionally, he was still working as a salesman, putting in seventy to eighty hours per week. But he wanted a different life for himself and his family.

The first year he spoke professionally, he had more than 200 bookings, but most of them were for free.

In time, he started getting paid to speak, and the rest, as they say, is history.

I think most of the readers of this book can achieve a level of speaking competence that will enable you to speak in a wide variety of business or personal situations where public speaking is required. Whether or not you will become a professional speaker, and get paid, and even paid well, or someone who achieves the level of excellence of Warren Greshes or other speakers I have heard that are truly amazing, like Larry Winget, remains to be seen. But work hard and practice what you learn in this book and from the other speaking-related reading and training that you open yourself up to, and see what happens. The sky's the limit for you as a speaker if you are willing to put in the time in front of audiences, learning what works for you and what you need to work on.

Warren Greshes shared some of his secrets for success with the audience of speakers that he was addressing. I considered the most important point he made in his forty-five minute presentation was that you have to practice your speech so that you know it so well that you can occasionally ad lib, what they used to call speaking "extemporaneously."

I know. You may be thinking that suggesting that someone practice his or her speech is patently obvious — a "no brainer," if you will — but there are many, perhaps even you are among them, who will give a speech without trying it out first, or who do not review their notes often enough so that all the key facts, figures, and anecdotes are committed to memory.

Warren Greshes suggested that you practice in front of the mirror or in front of your friends or family.

You can also practice by joining your local chapter of Toastmasters, an international membership organization that holds weekly meetings where members have a chance to speak in front of each other. Fortunately there are Toastmaster chapters throughout the world including twelve chapters in just the city of New Delhi, India. (If you go to http//www.toastmasters.org you will find a way to search for clubs anywhere in the U.S. There are also chapters in several cities in Nigeria; in Ho Chi Minh City in Vietnam; in Spain; in Turkey; or in India, where there are more than thirty chapters in Kolkata, Mumbai, and Chennai; as well as in Russia, where there are two chapters in Moscow and a chapter in St. Petersburg.) If there is no Toastmasters International chapter near you, you can always get together with a few other aspiring or seasoned speakers and start your own group.

With or without membership in a formal speaking club, however, reading *The Fast Track Guide to Speaking in Public,* and becoming more aware of public speaking by making an effort to attend the presentations of outstanding and first-rate professional speakers (or even getting the CDs or videos, or watching speeches at youtube.com of memorable speakers and viewing those materials), will take you far toward achieving your goal of becoming a more confident and competent public speaker — a key skill for those who are seeking leadership roles in a company, in a community, and in their society.

Thinking on your feet, one of the traits that admirable speakers have or develop, will help you with some of the activities related to speaking in public, namely, being interviewed on the radio, over the Internet, or on television. (You'll get some specific suggestions about how to improve your ability to do well in those types of speaking situations in Chapter 12, "Giving TV/Cable Media Interviews.")

Your starting point

So get ready to work on your speaking skills as you learn the secrets to speaking in public. If you don't have an example of a recent speech that you've given, take a few moments now to put your camera on a tripod and tape yourself giving a short speech in front of a group of friends, family, or colleagues, or, if you prefer, just by yourself, in front of the camera. You can study this sample and you can also use it to compare how your skills improve as you move forward in this book.

It is my goal that by reading this book you will develop the confidence to make good decisions about your speeches so you become the speaker you've always wanted to be. And if you are already speaking, and consider yourself to be a professional speaker, perhaps you will find at least a nugget or two in this book that reinforces what you are already doing or shows you a new way of doing things that might work differently or better for you.

Chapter 2
WHAT IT TAKES TO BE AN EXCELLENT SPEAKER

Have you gone to hear a speaker who was absolutely terrific? And, conversely, have you sat through the speech of someone with "marbles in his mouth" whose talk was disorganized, boring, and of little substance? I still remember clearly when, as a high school student, my older sister and I went from Queens, New York, where we lived, traveling almost two hours by public transportation to Manhattan to hear the novelist and philosopher Ayn Rand speak. She was commanding on the podium. She had a presence and a strength to her words that was exemplary. I found her spoken words were as powerful as the words in her novels *The Fountainhead* and *Atlas Shrugged.*

Of course, if you're introducing a colleague at an upcoming conference, or giving a forty-five minute keynote to a room full of eighth graders, you may not feel it's right for you to be judged by the same standards as the history-making speeches given by the great leaders of the last century, such as Winston Churchill, Jawaharlal Nehru, President John F. Kennedy, Mother Teresa, or Martin Luther King, Jr.! But, these "giants" certainly point to a level of speaking excellence worth aspiring to.

As Simon Sebag Monetfiore says in the introduction to the CD audio version of twenty-one speeches performed by their speakers that accompanies the book, *Speeches That Changed the World*: "A great speech captures the truth of its era whether its truth or its folly... These speeches teach us the power of words.... The finest speeches are generally not written by speechwriters or at least their essence is created by the person delivering the address."

Thinking over the speeches I've observed, as well as the reaction to those I have given, here are the skills that help the superb and memorable speakers to stand out from those who are forgettable:

1. Even if this is a written speech and the speaker has notes, the speaker does not need to read that material to the audience but instead speaks directly to each member of the audience, making eye contact, being clear in what he or she has to say.

2. The speech seems tailored to a specific group even if it is not. Somehow it just seems to "fit" either by having principles that apply in a universal way or doing background research into a specific audience so customized examples are included. If it was not possible to get to the audience in advance, as is often the case with a public speech or seminar, examples are elicited from the attendees as the speaker gives his or her talk, transforming the general principles into a more customized format.

3. Flexibility. Excellent speakers go with the flow if there is a question posed that shifts the talk in another direction, or if a time or room change has to be accommodated.

4. Having something important and fresh to say. Memorable speeches are not the "same old, same old."

5. Showing respect for the time and intelligence of each audience member, not talking "down" to the audience, no matter what their age or educational level.

6. Doing the necessary planning for each and every speech and not trying to show up and just "do it" without preparation.

7. Arriving on time and, if possible, even ahead of time so it's possible to pick up information about the audience or, if the personality of the speaker is comfortable with this approach, mingle with the audience.

8. Being accessible afterwards if there are any questions that need to be addressed one-on-one, and to be able to shake

hands and talk with the audience if that is a comfortable approach for the speaker.

9. Sharing even one thought, one idea, that is memorable and useful. Having one line that is a "take away" that attendees write down in their notes, or on their smart phones.

10. Making sure that whatever is promised in a write-up about a speech or in promotional materials related to the presentation lives up to those expectations.

11. Audiovisuals are worth taking the attention away from the speaker to focus on those materials.

12. Handouts are clear and useful, reinforcing or expanding what is explored in the speech.

13. The speaker uses a clear and loud voice.

14. He or she is dressed appropriately for the occasion and audience.

15. The speaker exudes confidence.

16. Stage fright, if it is present, is used to the speaker's advantage. It does not shut down the speaker's ability to think or to present.

17. Humility is a trait of great speakers.

18. Excellent speakers do not hype a product or themselves. If there is a reference to a product, including a book the speaker has authored or co-authored, it is done in a way that is comfortable and a natural extension of what is being said.

19. Memorable speakers are willing to share appropriate personal examples or anecdotes that will help the audience to learn from the speaker's mistakes and triumphs.

20. Making sure his or her presentation answers this question: "Did I do my best and did I provide information, inspiration,

and examples that made it worth my audience's time and money to listen to me for that speech/presentation?"

These twenty points are discussed in greater detail throughout this book.

Adult learning

When you speak, especially if you are speaking to adults, you have to consider the way that adults learn when you are preparing your speech. This may also impact on how you will present the material. The lecture approach, which you may have endured during your school years, is probably not going to work with those in your audiences. Understanding adult learning is one of the tools that will help you to become an excellent speaker.

The ASTD (American Society of Training and Development) Infoline booklet provides some of the characteristics of adult learners that teachers (and all speakers) need to consider:

1. Need is a motivator for the adult learner. How will the training help them?

2. What are the benefits of the learning?

3. What are the consequences of not learning?

4. Learning is enhanced through a variety of activities, rather than straight lecturing.

For adult learners, a more informal learning environment, such as a U-shaped seating arrangement, along with refreshments, may facilitate adult learning more than a traditional classroom setup. (For more details about room set-up, refer to Chapter 9.)

I took a three-day intensive seminar conducted by the ASTD, and one of the foci of that seminar was to understand the four steps in the training process: Purpose; Preparation; Presentation; Performance. I learned a great deal during those three days; one key concept is the establishment of a positive learning environment when you speak. You create such an environment by making sure that your attendees have the answers to the four key points that began this section.

Let everyone know that their opinion is valued and give the group time to share with each other by breaking out into smaller groups; facilitate more than you lecture; and include rewards in the learning experience. I still have the Certificate of Completion that I was given at the end of that training. How many of us have kept the giveaways from a conference or even from a particular speech we attended as a reward or a memento of that experience?

Today's speaking engagement, by and large, is quite different from the experiences that you had in your formative years and, depending upon your age now, how prevalent having a smart phone or another electronic device during your learning experience defined those speeches. I remember a few years ago I heard a keynote luncheon address to a group of several hundred writers by Peter Shankman, who created a free public relations tool called HARO (Help a Reporter Out). He actually suggested that everyone in that room *should* be tweeting on Twitter.com about the speech they were just hearing. He was making a point about how social media has changed the speed with which information is shared; he did not seem to consider such behavior by his audience as an insult to him as a speaker. Having those in your audience reading or sending text messages is more typical than ever before, so you might get used to it and deal with it rather than fight it and be offended by it. (Of course you can certainly ask your audience to shut off their smart phones and request their complete attention but try not to overreact if some are so addicted that it is hard for them to comply.)

So a big part of understanding adult learning today is being aware of who is in your audience and how they learn best. PowerPoint used to be standard in every presentation but it got too repetitive to see long sentences of text that basically outlined what the speaker was going to say. For a while, speakers tried not to use PowerPoint. As the PowerPoint guru and trainer Mike Landrum said in his presentation to speakers about more effectively using PowerPoint, the bad speakers got better by using PowerPoint but the better speakers had their presentations pulled down by the use/misuse of it. There is, however, a way to use PowerPoint that enhances a presentation. I will discuss that further in Chapter 9, "The Mechanics of Speaking."

For now, the key point to remember is that adults need to be motivated to learn and to stay engaged in the learning process. As a speaker, you want to keep your audience listening to you. It's a tall order. It's not an easy thing to do. The mind gets so easily distracted and wanders but if you are interesting, if you work hard at your presentation so that you "wow" them when you're in front of them, they *will* listen, they *will* respond, because when they *want* to learn, they really do!

Chapter 3
WHAT MAKES SPEAKING SUCH A UNIQUE WAY TO EDUCATE, INFORM, ENTERTAIN

Why speak?

Many who have picked up this book may be reading it because their answer to "Why speak?" is that their boss asked them to, or they have so much to share on a certain topic and they're not ready to put it all into a book yet.

The reasons for wanting to speak range from being asked to being compelled to do it. Yet, there are many in the speaking community who talk about "the calling." That they "have" to speak.

If you are one of those speakers who "has" to speak, there is no reasoning with you. It's like someone who "has" to write or "has" to paint. I feel that way about writing. When people ask me about whether or not it's difficult for me to write, I will usually answer, "It's hard for me *not* to write."

But whether you're driven to speak or you simply have to speak because someone asked you to and your job, or your relationship with that person remaining a positive one, depends on it, you want to be good — if possible, even excellent or brilliant — when you do speak.

That's going to take practice and hard work. Yes, just like you get better as a writer from writing, you get better as a speaker from speaking. And not all those speeches will be for money; in fact, in the beginning, most of your speeches may be for free.

To help you as you keep going on your journey to become a better speaker, listen to the words of Scott Crabtree, who discovered that he loved speaking so much that he quit his job of more than twenty years of making video games and software to become a full-time speaker on happiness. Here's what Scott Crabtree shared in an e-mail to me about the "why" behind this transformation:

> Speaking is the most rewarding thing I've ever done because I feel I can help people change their lives for the better. Too many of us plod through work, waiting for happiness after the job is done. Or we strive to achieve our goals, thinking success will bring us happiness. Science tells us we can make ourselves happy along the way. Studies tell us happiness brings success more than success brings happiness. I'm in love with the science of happiness and want to tell the world about it. Speaking gives me the chance to do that.
>
> Part of what makes it so rewarding is people telling me that my talks have changed their lives. Some tell me that I exposed them to the science of happiness (positive psychology, neuroscience, etc.) and they went on to learn more and put it into action. Some tell me little things, such as:
> - "We remembered to offer our boss fewer choices, so he was happier with the choice he made."
> - "I'm doing less multi-tasking now, and I get into 'flow' much more often. It's great!"[1]
> - Since learning from you that relationships are key to happiness, I'm investing in them more, with great success."

Scott Crabtree's enthusiasm for speaking reminded me of the speeches I gave to several classes of summer school students at a local elementary school. It was more than a decade ago but it seems like yesterday! They were attending summer school to improve their basic reading, writing, and math skills. I had been asked to speak about my journey to becoming a published author.

---

[1] Quotes not attributed to a published book are from private original communications between this author and the named speaker and are included in this book with permission.

In preparation for my presentation, I did some digging in my filing cabinets and I found my very first published writings, from fifth and sixth grade class magazines.

I used those writings in my speech by reading them to the students. Then I said something like, "Was that writing that great? Not really. I bet most of you can write as well or even better than I did. But what I did is that I wrote, and I kept writing, and I did a lot of reading, and I didn't give up on my dream."

I showed them my children's book, *The Cantaloupe Cat,* which was about to be published, and I showed them a couple of my other published nonfiction books for adults.

"You can be a professional writer if you want to be," I said to each student in those three separate classes.

I could see from the expressions on their faces that they were inspired and motivated by what I shared with them that day. I didn't act high and mighty, I didn't brag, I emphasized what they could do if they also wanted to become a writer. To write. To read. Not to be discouraged.

The next week, to my surprise, I received three sets of letters, some with drawings, from each of the classes; the students all thanked me in their own words for my presentation. I even got a letter from a girl who had not been there but had heard about my talk and she wrote to say she wished she had been present.

What I especially liked about those presentations is that I took the approach of empowering the students so they might become published authors if they wanted to be rather than dwelling on my own accomplishments and making it sound like I was better than them. And by reading my earliest writings, I was showing how much I was just like most of them. I also told them to make sure they kept their earliest work and not to leave it up to their parents to do that for them.I advised them to just put it some place where they could find it, in a notebook or in a file folder, because those writings are special and precious.

Dear Mrs. Yager,

Thank you for coming in to speak to us about
writing books. I enjoyed your visit and learned a lot.
It was my first time I saw an author in person. I
might want to be an author when I grow up.

Sincerely,

Sample "testimonial" letter from student who
attending my presentation on my writing career
(Name is intentionally concealed)

From a communication with me, Jeffrey Gurian shares the personal reasons behind his public speaking:

I stuttered very badly until I was in my 20's. I couldn't even say my name. My parents took me for speech therapy, but no one was able to help me. I came to realize that I didn't stutter when I was alone, which told me there was really nothing wrong with me. I was determined to conquer this problem. I wanted to be a doctor and a stuttering doctor does not inspire confidence in people. I also refused to go through my entire life with this disability if I was able to conquer it.

In my efforts, I made myself run for president of the freshman class at Hunter College. I even had other students introduce me to potential voters because I couldn't introduce myself. I told myself that if I could win the election I would no longer stutter since it would show me that people liked me. After all, you can't win an election if people don't vote for you.

I won the election but I still stuttered. It taught me the great lesson that outside validation doesn't work. It doesn't matter how many people tell you you're wonderful and fantastic, it only matters what you think of yourself.

Then I signed up for a speech class. Not therapy, a class where I would *have* to give speeches. I challenged myself and wanted to confront my fears. Lo and behold, it was amazing because even though I almost died of fright each time I had to give a speech, I didn't stutter. People were amazed. I stuttered before and after the speech but not during. What I figured out was that I "became someone else," like an actor does when he takes on a role in a movie. I became someone who wasn't nervous and didn't stutter.

Over the next few years I worked on myself, to the point where I speak perfectly. I basically took my mind apart and examined all of my thoughts about myself to determine which ones were no longer valid. I convinced myself that I no longer "needed" to stutter.

No one could ever tell that I stuttered, and I became many things all of which use speech. I became a successful Cosmetic Dentist, a professor at NYU in Oral Medicine-Oro-Facial Pain, and now I am a stand-up comedian, red carpet host, and I go on radio and TV all the time and work with some of the biggest stars in the business. I have an internet TV channel called "Comedy Matters TV" where I have 125 interviews with major celebs and I am on camera all the time and I don't stutter. I also teach stutterers my technique of how not to stutter, which is a great gift to me.

I want to get the message out to stutterers all over the world that there is hope for them and that it's not the kind of thing they have to suffer with for the rest of their life. All you have to do is embrace the role of someone who doesn't stutter and keep playing it.

So we've now looked at a couple of the reasons to speak. Scott Crabtree shared how it makes him feel useful spreading the message that anyone can become happier if they apply what we have learned from the happiness research. I shared that speaking allowed me to inspire and motivate those school children to want to be writers. Jeffrey Gurian's story gives stutterers hope.

Other reasons to speak? To share from your own experience so that others can learn from your triumphs and mistakes.

By speaking, you can also communicate your knowledge or specialized information about a specific topic, like how to cook or how to use social media to grow your business; or awareness about emotions or life experiences.

You can use speaking to influence opinion or to gather support for a candidate in an election, at school or in your local community. You can use speaking to plead your case whether you are asking for your beloved's hand in marriage, or you are given five minutes to explain why you would be the best person for a job.

From speech to book

There are numerous examples of speeches that have become books; as noted earlier, this book on public speaking began as a speech I gave seven years ago. My very first published book, *The Vegetable Passion: A History of the Vegetarian State of Mind,* published by Scribner's, actually started out as a speech that I gave to my college public speaking course when I was a junior.

A very famous live speech that first became a video and then a book, translated into more than forty languages, is *The Last Lecture,* by Randy Pausch, co-authored by Jeffrey Zaslow. You may have heard the story before, but it is a story that does bear repeating.

Randy Pausch was a professor of Computer Science, Human Interaction, and Design at Carnegie Mellon University. On September 18, 2007, Dr. Pausch, who had been diagnosed with terminal pancreatic cancer and told he had just three to six months to live, gave what came to be known as his last lecture on "Really Achieving Your Childhood Dreams." The video of that lecture did not deal with death. Rather, Pausch's lecture, in which he talked about his dreams and how he went about making those dreams happen, and his philosophies on life, got millions of views when it was broadcast on the Internet. There was humor in Pausch's lecture and present for it was fellow Carnegie Mellon University alumnus, *Wall Street Journal* columnist Jeffrey Zaslow. Author Zaslow collaborated with Pausch on a book version of that famous speech which was entitled *The Last Lecture;* it became an instant bestseller when it was first released. A year and a half later, on July 25, 2008, Pausch died from cancer but not without leaving the legacy for his three young children and for the world in his speech, captured on video, and in his book, *The Last Lecture*.

So consider turning your speech into a book. You could even use the speaking engagements to research and write each of the chapters of your book with each speech a different chapter. One of the benefits of using the speaking experience as the inspiration for a book is that you are getting active and priceless feedback from your audience into the ideas and concepts that you plan to put into your book. Your audience becomes almost a focus group, or way of testing out, your ideas but also getting valuable input from those who attend your speeches or workshops with their examples and anecdotes.

Of course be very cautious and careful about how you use any information that you do learn from your attendees, especially if it is a company-sponsored internal speaking event. If you have signed a non-disclosure agreement, you will not be able to use that material. And even if you did not sign a non-disclosure agreement, you need to show discretion and common sense about what you do with what you learn when you are speaking. Still, as long as you exercise good judgment and some caution, you are learning things that might not have been available to you without the exposure you are accorded because of your speaking engagement.

You might even consider planning for the research aspect of being a speaker by having a confidential questionnaire — keep it as short as possible — that you bring with you to distribute during your speech to help you get information that will be used in future speeches or a book. Especially if you have agreed to speak for free, the meeting planner may be very open to having you "poll" the audience since you are not getting compensated. I did this when I spoke as part of the spring lecture series of an educational group that had been meeting for many years in Cambridge, Massachusetts on the topic of "Risking Anger, Staying Friends." I distributed a one-page survey that was filled out by twenty-nine attendees. I made it very clear that participation was completely voluntary; a survey could be completed and returned anonymously or contact information could be provided in case I wanted to follow-up.

Practically every single person not only filled out the survey but they seemed quite thrilled to be sharing; it was cathartic for them to answer the first question, "when is the last time you wanted to express anger to a friend? Write down who it was and the circumstances related to it." After all, since the topic of my talk was, "Risking Anger, Staying Friends," those who paid to attend my presentation were predisposed to a concern about this topic. By filling out and returning their answer to that question plus four additional questions, as well as writing any additional comments in the "Use the space below" open-ended section of the questionnaire, the audience had the catharsis of being able to share about this topic and without having to do it publicly during the talk.

I plan to use the results from those questionnaires, along with follow-up communications or interviews, in the new book on friendship that I've been working on.

Entertaining

Last, but not least, you can use speaking to entertain whether or not you're a stand-up comedian or a singer or a juggler. Whether it is just you up there for forty-five minutes or you are a ten-minute relief speaker in between several intense panels on a complicated, specialized topic, speakers can make the audience cry out with laughter or sing along with enthusiasm.

Chapter 4
WHAT EVERY SPEECH AND SPEAKER NEEDS

E ssentially every speech has three components:

- An opening
- A closing
- What you share and reinforce in the middle

It's pivotal to start strong, and end strong, but you of course don't want to lose your audience in the middle, either!

Unlike writing a book, where you have pages and pages to work out your thesis and make your points, in a speech you have just those initial couple of minutes when you start talking to win over your audience.

The change in how an audience feels about listening to a speaker because of the Internet and the speed of learning and information distribution has led to a radical change in the way presentations begin today. This is reflected in the revised approach to introductions shared with me by the National Speakers Association, the professional association of speakers. When I was accepted to present a concurrent session on foreign rights at their annual meeting that was held in New York City a few years ago, I was informed that a biography of the speaker is no longer going to be a long, drawn-out list of accomplishments that starts the presentation. Instead, the speaker's bio would be included in the handouts for the session. The revised approach would be for the speaker to deliver useful content to the audience *within ninety seconds* of standing at the front of the room.

If you had a fear of speaking before, consider the pressure on you having to deliver something memorable in that first ninety seconds.

Just like the TV show that has to be so good you don't turn the dial to another program, when you start speaking you need to win over your audience so they feel they made a good choice deciding to spend their time (and often their money as well) to hear you speak.

Don't get scared or worried, however! In Chapter 7, "The Keynote," we'll look at how to develop a memorable ninety-second opener. Although that material will be related to creating, and delivering, a keynote speech — one of the most challenging speeches to give because it's usually just you and the audience and forty-five minutes (to an hour) to "wow" them — you will still want to have a powerful start to every speech you give, whether it's a full day seminar, a forty-five-minute "break out" session, or even the toast to the employee of the month that you've been asked to deliver.

Making that first ninety seconds "work" is an outgrowth of who you are as a speaker and your own background but it will also help if you get to know your audience so you can start off with something that will be especially appealing to that group of people. That means, if possible, getting to know your audience before you appear in front of them as a speaker. This topic is explored, with some suggestions about how to find out more about your audience, in the section that follows.

Getting started

In Chapter 1 I asked you to create a short video of yourself speaking or to find a recent recording of you making a presentation. Now take a few moments now to review that video. That's your starting point. Do you look confident? Is your voice loud enough? Do you have enough enthusiasm, too little, too much? What topic did you choose to speak on for this sample? Are there any memorable ideas or phrases or words in what you said? Did you use storytelling, statistics, or a famous quote to make a point?

How will you prepare the speech you have to give?

In Chapter 7, "The Keynote," I discuss the opening, middle, and ending of a speech in greater detail. Right now, however, it is just useful to know that in order to be "extemporaneous," meaning you seem as if you are speaking "off the top of your head," you have to do a lot of preparing so you can seem spontaneous!

There are three basic ways to do that:

- The outline method
- The key word only approach
- Writing out your entire speech

All three methods have pluses or minuses and you also do not have to use one method all the time. I tend to go back and forth between the outline or keyword methods, and the writing out the entire speech approach. And I tend also to use a fourth method, which is a hybrid of the other three: I write out the speech, and then I do an outline based on that written out speech, and then I also make notes or jot down key words for myself that I will have available to me "just in case" so that if I need a specific quote or example that I may have memorized, the notes are "back up" if I need it.

Writing out the speech and then writing an outline, followed by notes or key words, is for me the best way to be able to be extemporaneous when I actually deliver the speech but still be organized and knowledgeable.

I have mentioned that it is possible to turn a speech into a book or even an article. If you use the written out method of speech preparation, that is more likely to happen. That written out speech just might become the first draft of your article or a couple of chapters in a book. You can, of course, still turn an outline for a speech into the basis of a book but the written out material will give you a "jump start" on the writing process.

Is it okay to read some or all of your speech when you present? There are no "rules" although, of course, the more you don't have to read from a sheet of paper, or a teleprompter, usually the better. But you have to use your judgment, of course, and be flexible, because if your speech calls for it, reading something to your audience can be the most powerful part of your speech. For example, I gave a talk on friendship a few years ago as the keynote speaker to a fundraiser luncheon for an association in New Jersey. I outlined the speech and was able to speak without any notes for the entire speech until I came to the ending. I had determined that the best way to end my presentation would be to share a poem I had written called "Friendshifts," the same name as the title of my book, *Friendshifts*. The poem was 4-1/2 pages long, too long for me to memorize.

I read the poem, looking up, of course, often, still making eye contact, putting animation into my voice. The poem was the kind of poem that told a story and I felt that powerful and wonderful feeling that we are honored to get as speakers when the audience is "with us," listening to, hanging on to, our every word. And I ended the speech, as I ended the poem, with these words,

"Yes, friendshifts happen
And that's okay
As long as you have at least one good friend
To sit in that chair next to you
So none of us ever have to be alone
Unless we want to be."

During the break that followed, many audience members came up to me to tell me how much my presentation meant to them, and I sold ninety-eight copies of the book, so I knew they not only were moved by my talk but also wanted to read/learn more.

Who is your audience?

I was fortunate that the meeting planner for that luncheon sent out cards to everyone who registered for the lunch and they asked everyone to write on the back of the card one question about friendship that they wanted me to answer. They were instructed to "turn your card in at the door."

Of course it would have been nice to have gotten the cards a few days, or even hours, in advance of my speaking engagement, but even getting those cards right before my talk gave me time to quickly review the cards and to make sure I knew what the expectations were for the audience so I could try to meet those goals with the talk I had planned. And if there were some real surprises in what everyone wanted to hear about, I could make those changes as well. Fortunately, the questions they wanted me to answer were the ones I had pretty much already prepared to address but it was still useful to have that audience involvement even before I started to speak.

If you have the opportunity to send out a pre-speech audience survey, you can do that.

In the Appendix is a sample audience questionnaire that you can send out, by e-mail or by mail, or you can even create a survey in the online program that I've used for various surveys over the year, www.surveymonkey.com sending the website or url for your survey to the attendees of your upcoming speech.

Here are some of the basic questions to ask:

> Name (optional)
> Company (optional)
> Location
> What is the #1 issue that you are hoping to have this speech address?
> Have you heard other presentations on this topic before?
> If yes, what were those presentations and when did you hear them?
> Anything else about yourself or about this upcoming speech that you'd like to share that might be helpful to me in my preparations so this is as useful a speech to you as possible?
> Please return this pre-speech questionnaire by e-mail, fax, or by mail. You can keep this questionnaire completely anonymous or you can share your contact information in confidence.
> Please also indicate if you are open to follow-up communications by phone or e-mail and, if you are, how to get in contact with you and the best time(s) to reach you.

Thank you in advance and I look forward to seeing you in the near future.

Here are seven ways that I've used to find out about an audience before a speech:

1. Interview the person who asked you to speak.

    Talk on the phone if you are unable to meet and talk in person. Ask her what kind of people you can expect to have in your audience. What are their concerns? What does he or she think they will expect to get from your presentation? If it's a nonfiction topic, are there any recent, past, or future events that caused her or him to ask you to speak (such as changes at the company, in the industry, at the association)? If you interview this person right away, try to interview him or her at least once more in the week or two prior to your speech.

2. Interview audience members in advance.

    How do you manage to do that? Here's what London-based speaker and media expert Alan Stevens shares about why finding out as much as possible about your audience is so important and how to go about it:

    > Whatever kind of speech you are delivering, and *especially* if you are speaking to a breakout session at an association conference, you need to do some research on your audience. Many speakers spend a lot of time researching their topic, which is clearly important, but the ultimate judges of success will be the people in your audience. If they have an area of special interest, you need to know what it is, find out what are their concerns, and then offer them valuable advice.
    >
    > How do you find this out? A few weeks before the event, ask the organizer to provide you with contact details for likely audience members. Contact them and ask about their concerns. It's that simple.

3. Conduct a short survey of any registrants who have indicated that they are willing to answer written questions in advance of the speech.
   If possible, also do a follow-up interview via e-mail, phone, or in-person.

4. If you are speaking before a particular company, visit the company's website.
   Read their annual report. Speak to as many employees as possible as well as someone in human resources. Read articles written about the company.

5. Arrive half an hour early to speak and as soon as attendees start arriving, distribute to them a short questionnaire and have everyone fill it out before you even begin your talk.
   Collect their completed questionnaires and read them right there on the spot, before you begin speaking. Ask a few key questions:

   • Name
   • Occupation
   • What is your #1 goal for my speech
   • What would you like to share about yourself that would help me get to know what your expectations are for my speech?
   • Have you attended any other speeches related to the topic of today's speech? If yes, what there those speeches?

6. Don't worry about getting to know your audience in advance; find out more about them right at the speaking engagement.
   This is another option but it has to be used carefully and with judgment. You don't want to walk into a room of salesman with lots of anecdotes related to acting or travel writing.
   But if you are especially strapped for time, it is possible to use some of the time you have at the beginning of the speech, before you plunge into the key ideas you want to share that are so general and basic that those ideas, with just some

modification, will fit most any audience, to get your audience to share with you about themselves, so you find out about them right then and there.

7. If you have asked for a flip chart and markers, and if your audience consists of one-hundred or fewer so that the flip chart could be seen, you can also write down the answers as the answers are shared. Here are some sample questions that you might ask:

- What is your greatest challenge right now around _____ (*fill in with whatever topic you were asked to speak on, such as sales, dealing with coworkers, public speaking, using social media, increasing the number of clients you have, etc.*)
- What is the Number One piece of technology that you find useful in getting your job done?
- If you could change one thing about your job, what would it be?
- What is distinctive about your company compared to other industries that you would want an industry outsider to know about your job?
- (In community, not work-related situations): What sets your association (or club) apart from all the others that individuals could join?
- What has your club (or association) accomplished this year that makes you the most proud?

The audience is part of your world forever. Your connection does not have to end when the speech ends.

That's what makes speaking so unique, compared to writing. You have the opportunity to engage your audience not just when you are speaking but in an ongoing way. Of course writers can do that as well with readers who write to the author and who become fans by attending author events or reading other works by the same author or even sending tweets or e-mails with comments about their writing.

But it's a different way of interacting than it is with the audience who hears a speech and can engage in a dialogue with the speaker, right then and there.

Getting your audience involved

Some time ago I went to a presentation with around 1,000 people in the room and the presenter was consultant, business guru, and author Marshall Goldsmith. After all these years, I still remember what he did: he got the 1,000 people in the audience to participate. Yes, participate. This is memorable because, until that point, people would say to me, "You can't have audience participation if there are more than fifteen in a workshop," or something like that, thereby putting a number limit on whether or not you could use audience participation in your speech.

But here was Marshall Goldsmith using audience participation with an audience of more than 1,000 and how did he do it? The answer is so obvious it's embarrassing I hadn't seen it that way before. He had everyone turn to the person to their right (or their left) and suddenly there were five-hundred or so pairs of two. You can always have audience participation if there's a pair to work with.

Now let's get to the reason for having audience participation (as well as, if time permits, and it seems like a good idea for that particular speech, a Q&A — question and answer session — toward the end of the speech). There are actually multiple reasons. The first is that, as this example from that presentation by Marshall Goldsmith shows, we tend to remember more based on what we do than on what we hear.

One of the audience participation exercises I like to use when I give a keynote or do a workshop is to ask the audience to find someone in the room who is a total stranger and to go over to that stranger and spend three minutes sharing about themselves. And to find at least three things they have in common. This works well as an ice-breaker but it also fits in very nicely with one or more of the topics I speak on, work relationships and also friendship. It shows that connections can start in almost any situation, if you just have the opportunity. It also shows that total strangers usually have multiple things in common if they look for those similarities.

The book, *Tellin' Ain't Training* (see the References for details) is one of those great book titles that is so powerful and moves your mind to such a new place that it almost replaces the necessity of having to read the book. (Of course the authors who worked so hard to write some 180+ pages of information probably won't agree that their title "says it all!")

Many speakers will invite their audience to contact them with feedback or comments, or just to stay connected. Some of those speakers are sincere in that offer. Some just do it because it sounds nice at the time, only to ignore those offers when audience members do actually follow up.

My suggestion is that you do not make such an offer unless you intend to follow up on it. Don't make your words hollow and untrue. Mean it if you say it. And, yes, if 10% of an audience of two-hundred follow up directly, it will be a lot of individualized back and forth so decide in advance if it's worth it to you.

The sooner you take in the audience as a key part of your speaking engagement, the better it will be for you as a speaker and in any of the related careers that brought you to your speaking role in the first place whether that's as a writer, academic, business executive, entrepreneur, small business owner, or association director.

Don't be like the book publisher who would like to find a way to publish books without needing authors, or film directors who would like to make a movie without actors and actresses. (They just "tolerate" those parts of the "process;' but they really prefer their "own" kind.)

The audience, rather than something to be feared and resented, is a part of the speaking experience that makes it what it is and it can even become the best part of it.

If dealing with the audience is especially hard for you, you might want to consider taking a course in social networking or even in communication skills. It is a question of personality as well as an art and a skill and becoming more comfortable interacting with your audience is going to serve you well as a speaker.

Using your voice

It may seem obvious, but this is something every speaker has to consider. Beyond the words that you are saying — and I discuss how pivotal it is to start with the right ideas and then the right words to express those ideas in the next chapter on the twelve secrets to great speaking — is *how* you are saying those words. The "how" includes any accents you might have that will make it more challenging for the audience to understand you, based on who is in the audience and how familiar they are with your particular accent, as well as how loud you are and how clearly you enunciate or articulate your words.

If you have challenges with any of those components of how you speak, work on your own or with a speech or speaking coach to improve your capabilities. Of course, as noted in Chapter 9 on "The Mechanics of Speaking," having a working microphone can make a big difference in whether you are heard in the back of a huge auditorium. But even with the best sound system, if you are slurring your words, or are too soft spoken, what could have been a powerful and memorable speech or workshop might instead be a frustrating experience for your audience and an even more disappointing experience for you because your ideas and words will not be heard let alone considered or acted upon.

Using your voice also means using silence to your advantage. I remember years ago going to a speaking presentation by the NSA Chapter in New York City. I can't remember who the speaker was who made that point but I do remember the point because it was demonstrated by having silence and seeing what it did to the presentation.

Think of that concept. "We will now pause for a moment of silence." It is a way that we draw attention to a thought or a shared experience that a group is collectively memorializing such as a moment of silence to remember those who have passed away.

Putting even a moment or two of silence into your presentation, to make a point, and at the right time, can be powerful. It will also prevent the audience from seeing you as a non-stop "choo-choo train" of words and speaking.

Making eye contact

This is another way to use yourself to connect with your audience so you get your ideas, message, and information out to them beyond just the words you are saying. Making eye contact with your audience is of course one of the reasons why it is so much harder to connect when you are doing a webinar over the Internet, or a teleseminar over the phone, or you are speaking in such a huge venue and your audience is so large or the lighting is so bright that you cannot even see beyond the front row.

But if it is possible to make eye contact with some or all of your audience, it should result in a better speaking experience for you and a more connected listener event for your audience.

Here is a system that Frans Reichardt, a professional speaker and customer relations consultant based in Amsterdam, explains in an original communication with me about how he learned about the power of making eye contact and the system that he uses:

> It was only after so many years of public speaking that I learned one thing that really turned out to be an eye-opener. Literally. I consider it to be one of the secrets of successful speaking. Any speaker can do it and it always works. I love to share it with you.
>
> During a course I taught I used a simple technique to connect to the audience. This technique is: look them in the eyes!
>
> I remember how our teacher asked my fellow speakers and me to speak and at the same time look in the eyes of a person in the audience. Not just for a second, but for a couple of seconds before we switched to another person in the audience. That was not as easy as you might think it would be. Most of us are simply not used to looking a stranger in the eyes for more than just a second. Is it because we are taught it can be considered to be too intimate, rude or offensive to look a stranger straight in the eyes for too long?

Still that's what we had to do. And we had to do it again and again. At first it made us feel uncomfortable. Until we felt we connected to the person we looked in the eyes. Feedback from the audience also taught us they felt connected to the speaker much more than before. It worked for both parties involved: both speaker and audience!

I use this small trick to make sure I cover the whole audience. I start looking at someone on the left, than in the middle, than on the right. After that I look at someone in the front and then I pick someone in the back. Or the other way around. As long it is a cross shape movement.

Using body language

As you probably know by now, a fraction of what we learn about something or someone is the words they say. The bulk of it is the non-verbal — how someone stands, the loudness or softness of someone's voice, their dress, gestures, and pausing or silence, as mentioned above.

Speakers are trained to look at the non-verbal cues of their audience to pick up on how their ideas or words are being received, and to ascertain the mood of the audience, as a way of judging if the speech is resulting in boredom, joy, anxiety, or even rage.

But you also want to put a spotlight on your own body language and what you are telling the audience by the way you stand, what you are wearing, if your hands are folded across your chest, indicating that you are protecting yourself and even feeling unapproachable, or if you are standing straight and tall, and confident, but not aloof.

You don't want to let the audience know if you're afraid, so consider what messages you are sending out through your body language as well as your gestures, tone of voice, pauses, and silences. This will be discussed further later on.

Chapter 5

12 SECRETS FOR GIVING A TERRIFIC SPEECH

I want to offer you a succinct way to jump start your speaking career — and your confidence — by highlighting what I see as the twelve key secrets to becoming an excellent speaker.

Secret #1: It starts with your ideas.

Forget for now about the words you will use, or the props you might use to surprise your audience. You first step is to figure out the views and the thoughts you want to share. What is your vision of the world? Do you want to inform? To persuade? What do you want to say in your speech? What is it that you want your audience to know?

"Mr. Gorbachev, tear down this wall," said President Ronald Reagan at the beginning of that immortal speech. Those are the words that are always quoted because they contain the essence of the pivotal idea behind President Reagan's longer speech.

You need to keep up your research, even if that research is just observing people and being aware of changes in the world. You cannot allow your ideas to get stale or you will have stale speeches.

You can have the best technical speaking skills in the world — a voice that projects loud and clear to the back of the room, you can exude confidence on the podium, you can know how to "work the audience" so you make eye contact and they seem to like you and to hang on your every word — but if the ideas you have to share aren't exciting, cutting edge, unique, powerful, and memorable, none of those presentation skills will matter. It all starts with what you have to say and for some, that is sharing their own story, through storytelling, and for others, it is by offering statistics or information that the audience won't easily find anywhere else.

Whether you have five minutes or forty-five, three hours or three days, make those minutes or hours count. Give your audience one or more "take-aways" that they didn't have when they first walked into that room, or turned on the computer to take your webinar, and you will be a one-of-a-kind speaker who is fresh, valuable, and changing the world, one listener at a time.

In his classic book, *The 7 Habits of Highly Effective People*, Stephen R. Covey has this as the second habit: "Begin with the End in Mind."

Adapting Covey's concept to finding out the secrets of speaking in public is that you should prepare your speech with your audience in mind. And, even closer to Covey's concept, is that you should prepare your speech with a consideration about what you want your audience to take away from your speech.

When you are asked to speak, you also want to be clear about what you are supposed to speak about. This may sound obvious, but sometimes there is a disconnect between the topic that the speaker prepares and the topic that the meeting planner — or whoever is in charge of writing down and distributing the topic or title of the speech — tells the audience through the program or even an interoffice memo that you will speak on.

You might think that it should not matter. That a good speech is a good speech, no matter what. But having a match between the topic you are asked to speak on and what the audience comes to hear is the first step toward a satisfied audience and a positive speaking experience.

Secret #2: After ideas, it's the articulation of those ideas that counts whether it is put into concrete form as an outline or a written speech.

A speech has to have a beginning, middle, and end, and it's that much easier to do it on your feet if you've first done it on paper or on your computer, even if it's just an outline.

The same thing that makes for good writing makes for good speechwriting, namely, having a strong opening, telling examples, and a powerful ending.

If your written speech or outline is dull and boring, it's going to be hard to turn that into a captivating speech when you deliver it.

In screenwriting, they say that if it's not on the page, it's not on the screen. In speechwriting it's a similar concept: although you can of course be extemporaneous or ad lib to some extent, the basic approach to what you're going to be saying is probably best worked out in your outlined or written speech. That doesn't mean that you're going to read your speech, although some speakers find they need to stick to their written speech if they are to stay on track. For some, PowerPoint, discussed in a later chapter, helps to keep those speakers who need "reminders" on track. Announcers who are doing the evening news usually use teleprompters, a technique that allows them to see what they have to say without the audience/viewers knowing that they're "reading."

Speakers who use PowerPoint in settings where the screen is behind them may have a similar set up; they look at a teleprompter so they are able to "see" their PowerPoint without turning their back on their audience.

If you are a writer, you have an advantage over other speakers who are not writers. You can write a speech because you know how to put good writing together. You also know something that, unfortunately too few speakers know: excellent writing usually requires one or multiple rewrites. It doesn't just "happen." In order to get your speech, or writing, to the point that you want it to be, you have to keep writing and rewriting till it's "there."

Here's something that is the biggest secret of all in public speaking: you can hire someone to write a speech for you.

Speechwriting is a different skill from other kinds of writing. It is one of the most challenging types of writing and speechwriters typically command very big fees, or salaries if they are on staff for an executive or a government company or agency.

You can, of course, hire a freelance speechwriter. Or you can write the draft of your speech and hire someone to "tweak" it or edit it or make it stronger and better.

The costs in hiring a speechwriter can range from just below $100 for a speech or "tweaking" a speech that is already written, to several thousand dollars. It is an option to consider unless you feel you absolutely have to be "the one" to have written each of your spoken words. But keep in mind that it is possible to hire a professional speechwriter, someone who has a way with words, a way that you might lack.

But you can't hire someone to deliver your speech for you. I remember the scandal when a book publisher a couple of decades ago attempted to hire a stunning actress to do the media interviews for an author's book because the author was not as glamorous or media "friendly." It backfired big time because the public felt they were being deceived.

Although the audience and the media would like to believe that all speakers write all the words they speak, and it is ethical to disclose if a speech has had a speechwriter writing the whole thing, or doing a rewrite, it is certainly a possibility to consider if you just don't have the writing skills to create a road map for your speech that is going to be memorable and distinctive.

Obviously if you are giving a motivational speech, rather than just an informative one, your style and content may be different than if you are there to educate, but the basics of excellent public speaking are the same: be clear, interesting, and memorable.

This rule applies whether you are giving a toast at your best friend's wedding or speaking before an audience of three hundred on your area of expertise.

Secret #3: After getting what you are going to say "down on paper," focus on how you say it.

Here is where the performers, those with powerful presentation skills, will distinguish themselves from those who die on the platform.

To some extent, this is a natural inclination but the good news is that it is possible to improve your presentation skills.

Studying improvisation might help you to become more spontaneous and confident in how you appear in front of a group. Check out your local community offerings to see if there is an improvisation group that you could observe or even take lessons with or become part of.

Even if you don't plan to become a professional stand-up comedian, studying stand-up comedy might help you with your comfort level in front of an audience.

Work with a coach to get better in front of an audience.

Take a public speaking class.

As mentioned several times throughout this book, consider joining the local chapter of Toastmasters or a speaker association in your community or country, such as the National Speakers Association or the Asia Professional Speakers Association – Singapore. (See the Resource section for more listings.)

Secret #4: Know your audience.

We discussed this in the previous chapter. Here, in review, are a couple of suggestions: You can find out about your audience in advance, by doing a pre-speech survey; you can ask the meeting planner to share with you about their association and/or the audience; if it's a public seminar, and you won't be able to find out who is attending in advance, you can use the time when you first start your talk or after your opening to ask the audience to share with you by a show of hands. (Some more electronically savvy associations or companies, as well as those with big enough budgets, are renting audience polling systems that enable attendees to answer questions with a handheld device, with the answers being tabulated and shown on a screen right then and there. This can be useful if a company is trying to see trends from their employees and it is better to keep their responses anonymous and confidential even if they are in a room full of other attendees/employees.)

Secret #5: Prepare an introduction about yourself in advance.

Establish the answer to "Why me?" You may have an amazing reputation within certain circles, but you need to let your new audience know why you are the right person to share with them. Being a speaker is an honor and it is not an honor to be taken lightly. The best way to establish your credibility is to have an introduction that highlights your accomplishments related to this particular speech so that the audience starts off feeling lucky to be listening to you. You want to avoid having even one member of that audience wondering, "Why is this guy (or this gal) talking to me? *I* could be up there!")

If possible, do not leave your introduction to chance. If you go to the extensive website of professional speaker Warren Greshes, you will find, in the "Press Pack" part of the site, that you can download the bio about Warren that the person introducing Warren could use before he speaks.

If you do not yet have a sample introduction at your website, consider writing one and e-mailing it in advance to the person who is going to introduce you. Bring a physical copy of the preferred introduction along with you just in case the meeting planner or whoever is going to introduce you forgets to bring his/her copy.

Have an introduction to you and your speech that has the audience "on your side" from the get-go, that you are the right person to be speaking to them.

However, remember my example from the instructions I received when I was presenting before fellow speakers on foreign rights at the National Speakers Association annual meeting: no lengthy introductions. Get to the heart of the speech within ninety seconds. So be careful about how you handle this introduction issue. It should fit the length and tone of the group you are speaking to.

Secret #6: Be prepared.

This secret is a "no brainer" but it bears repeating: Be prepared. Do your homework. Whether you write your speech out and then learn it from that written out version or you use the outline method — the pros and cons of both methods are discussed in this book —

know your material. Avoid trying to "wing it" because those who are unprepared are usually the ones who find speaking terrifying or do not share enough that is fresh and new with their audience to make the audience feel grateful that they listened.

You probably know the old joke, "How do you get to Carnegie Hall?" that amazing concert hall in Manhattan, and the punch line to the joke is, "practice, practice, practice."

That's what you have to do to get better at speaking. Not just speaking in general, but presenting a specific speech.

This may not be as easy to do as you think. Many of us don't like to hear the sound of our own voice even though we love to speak. We don't like to look at videos of ourselves speaking, or even in family movies, even though we love to present or even to go on television and to be interviewed.

Get over it! You need to practice to improve your speaking skills.

If possible, practice out loud, but at least practice in your mind.

You need to practice in front of the mirror.

You need to practice in front of an audience.

You need to videotape yourself and play back the tape and look it over to see what works and what needs work in your presentation.

The more you practice a speech in advance of giving it, the more you can depart from your written speech or notes and ad lib and let the magic of the moment happen.

Practice doesn't necessarily make perfect but practice makes for more confidence.

Here is what that great speaker and meeting planner Dottie Walters and her daughter Lilly Walters wrote about practicing in their classic work, *Speak and Grow Rich:*

> To be paid for your performances and to keep getting more bookings, you must be very good on stage. This is the bottom line in professional speaking. You can ensure that you will be your best and in better control of your fears if you use the power of good preparation. Rehearse not only physically, but in the auditorium of your mind. Hear the roar of the crowd, the laughter, and the applause. Smile and turn to those friendly faces in your imaginary

audience as you mentally deliver each punch line. Grin back at them. When it is time to perform your program before your real audience, you will exude confidence.

If possible, get feedback before you give your speech. That will help you to revise your presentation so you are the best you can be. Where can you get feedback? You can work with a coach and that coach will give you feedback. You can perform your speech in front of an audience of friends and family and see what they say. But if the topic you are speaking on is not what your family or friends will respond to, it might be useful to at least speak in public but it might not give you the feedback you need.

Find out if a professional speaker or communications expert is giving a workshop that includes performance time, which could provide you with some professional input that is more affordable than the cost of working one-on-one with a coach.

Becoming a member of your local Toastmasters.com chapter is another way to get practice speaking, as well as feedback.

Until recently, stand-up comics practiced in front of an audience for free. It has become harder for them to do this because someone in the audience might have a camera in their phone and what was supposed to be a practice session suddenly shows up on www.youtube.com for all the world to see. But if you don't think you have to worry about that kind of notoriety yet, you can put together an audience for whom you will try out your "material" for free and get their feedback.

Secret #7: Share about yourself if it is comfortable and appropriate and if it fits the speech you are giving.

Audiences usually like to hear at least an anecdote or two about their speaker especially if it relates to the topic at hand but avoid making the entire speech about you. Use personal anecdotes in the service of your speech. Be in control of how much you share about yourself, and why you are sharing, rather than sharing too much because you did not prepare enough other material or you share about yourself out of nervousness.

The personal and professional anecdotes you share are often the strongest concepts that your audience will remember. But it needs to be part of your speech, nuggets of wisdom and experience that other examples and ideas reinforce or contrast so it is more than about "you." A speaker who did this in a very powerful way was the award-winning downhill ski racer, Bonnie St. John, who spoke to experts in the field of conflict resolution at a conference in Atlanta. I was a fellow speaker but I took the time to enjoy hearing Bonnie St. John, who was the keynote luncheon speaker, share her message about perseverance.

Although her own anecdotes about the challenges she faced, and overcame, as a young girl and then a woman with just one leg resonated with the audience, she presented her own experiences in a way that could be applied to any situation not just the example of falling down during the competition and taking too long to get up, which caused her to go from first to third place. As she used that experience to share her principle that it is not if you fall down that matters but how long you take to get back up it was clear that everyone in the audience, including me, could apply that insight into their own personal and career situations beyond skiing or sports.

Secret #8: Get the audience involved.

This concept is embraced in the bestselling book, *Telling Ain't Training* by Harold D. Stolovitch and Erica J. Keeps, as well as by the American Society of Training and Development (ASTD), which offers courses and training. It's a simple but powerful concept and it speaks to the trend that encourages speaks to engage their audience in the experience of learning so that you do not just have a speaker at the front of the room "telling" what is true.

This is an excellent concept and, in general, it will help take a speech that is okay and make it even more powerful.

But there is a caveat. In some cultures — whether corporate or geographical — the technique of having audience members share with each other or with the entire group their thoughts or experiences related to the topic at hand might backfire. The audience feels that they have come to hear the speaker — the expert — and not their uninformed peers.

Secret #9: Never let them know you're scared or feeling insecure.

There's a well-known phrase that started out as an ad campaign by Gillette Company for its antiperspirants. The slogan first introduced in 1984 was, "Never let them see you sweat."

That's a great slogan for your speaking engagements whether it's your first, fortieth, or hundredth speech.

After all, you are supposed to be someone who is seasoned in speaking in public or should not be up there in front of others in the first place. Avoid apologizing profusely about how unprepared you are or how flattered you are that you were asked to speak (although of course you want to thank the appropriate persons for giving you the opportunity). But you need to be up in front of that audience, whether it is six fellow coworkers or four-hundred total strangers, because you earned being up there. It is an example of the self-fulfilling prophecy. If you dwell on how you don't feel that you are up to the task of speaking, even if you are brilliant, your audience will pick up on your insecurity and doubt if they should bother listening to you at all.

Let the adrenaline you may be feeling work for you, not against you. That adrenaline will make you more animated and powerful. Telling everyone that you are scared will backfire.

Harness your fear by giving the best speech you can. Fortunately by reading about public speaking, and practicing more, by the time you speak for the first time, or each time after that, you will be a little less fearful and you will *never* be unprepared, even if you just have ten minutes to collect your thoughts and jot down a few ideas of what you will cover in your speech because you've been asked to present on very short notice.

Put your heart into your speech and try to enjoy the experience because the audience will know if you're happy to be there or in a state of fright. Based on my observations and first-hand speaking experiences over more than four decades, I think there is a direct relationship between how you feel about yourself when you walk into that room to speak and how the audience feels about you. If you are feeling confident and joyful, it will come through and the audience will be more inclined to like you and, by association, to enjoy spending time with you in that room.

If you're angry, stressed out, fearful, or worried about what everyone else thinks, rather than focused on pleasing yourself, that will show too, and it will backfire. The very crowd you are trying to please will reject your over-reliance on them for your affirmation. Instead, affirm yourself and you will be amazed at how much better your speaking engagements will go.

Secret #10: Give the speech you want to hear.
This is the speaking and speech version of the advice writers usually get, and that I have tried to live by, namely, write the book you want to read, so give the speech you want to hear especially if it's motivational or inspirational. If you are speaking on a specific topic for a very specialized audience, you may have to modify this concept to: give the speech that your audience needs to hear.

Whether you are speaking on a general theme or something targeted to that group, put yourself in the shoes of your audience. If you were in that audience, what would you want a speaker to share with you?

This is different than relying on your knowledge of the audience to help you to craft your speech. Giving the speech you would want to hear means that you take what you have learned about your audience and you consider your own likes and dislikes as well and you put that all together so you create a speech that you would want to hear but that is tempered by the needs of your audience.

Remember that your audience is not you. Even if you are speaking to your peers, the fact that you're up there in front of your audience does not take away from you being "one of them" but by being in the front of the room, by being the speaker, you are in a position of power and authority. You are the leader.

Your peers or not, your audience, whoever that audience is, is looking to you to provide one or all of the five "I's" of memorable speaking:

1. Information
2. Insight
3. Illumination
4. Interest
5. Inspiration

Information

What can you share that your audience hasn't heard before? Or, if it's familiar information, how can you say it in a way that is fresh and powerful?

Insight

What unique point of view can you share that they will take with them forever? If "everyone" thinks or acts a certain way, what have you done differently that they will remember forever? As noted earlier, keynote speaker Bonnie St. James, a woman who lost a leg to cancer, was determined to become a contender in the Olympic skiing competition, and she did. She didn't give up or dwell on her disability and she even chose a sport that relied on the very part of her body that she had lost. What an insight she gave to the idea of determination!

Illumination

This aspect helps to shed a light on something that your audience may have ignored before, or been clueless about, because you, the speaker, are now making associations and "connecting all the dots" that the audience might not have seen without your input.

Interest

You are interesting because isn't that what you expect from a speaker when you're in the audience?

You might even be an entertainer. Jana Stanfield, who is a singer and a speaker, delivers presentations that are powerful and memorable. On occasion, I've played songs if it seems like it might "work" with a specific audience.

There are speakers who are also magicians. That's a skill that might be cultivated if you think it would raise the interest level at your speeches.

There are speakers who are jugglers.

Others are humorists and that's how they keep the interest in their presentations.

I don't tell jokes, per se, but I do put humor into my presentations as a natural outgrowth of my topic. But it's important if you do use humor that you don't do it at the "expense" of any audience member or even any group. That would get you the reputation of being a "verbal bully" and even if you got a laugh or two initially at your presentation, you would develop a negative reputation that would not be in your best interest.

So if you do inject humor into your speeches, or tell a joke, don't do it at the expense of others especially disadvantaged groups who can be an "easy" target for a quick joke, and be careful to avoid jokes that take pot shots at celebrities. Such international comedians as Jimmy Fallon or *The Tonight Show's* Jay Leno might be able to get away with it, but that's what they do and that's who they are.

There are different rules for them. The typical speaker would not be in that category and your entertainment value has to come from a source other than making fun of others, whether they're celebrities, politicians, or sports figures.

Inspiration
Hardest to explain but you know when you've achieved it: sharing cutting edge information, touching hearts, and motivating change.

Secret #11: Learn from what went right and what went wrong so next time you are even better.

Of course no one likes rejection and we all want to be loved but we also need to grow and learn and we do that by figuring out what went right when we speak and what didn't go so well and could use some improvements.

I remember once I tried singing at the end of a presentation on time management to a room of paralegals. Fortunately I read through each and every evaluation because the reaction to my ending song was quite dramatically both positive and negative. It wasn't universally negative, so it showed me that since about three quarters of the attendees liked my song, I needed to decide if it was worth going along with the one quarter who thought it "ruined" my presentation or just go for the majority ruling.

Since that time, I tend not to end a presentation with a song, especially asking the audience to sing along, which is what I did with that group. But I had the courage to experiment with that song and with that technique and it showed me the risks of trying something new but also something that I had not gotten the training for if I really did want to make it work.

Have you spoken and had some or all of the experience a disappointment? Or have you spoken and everyone thought you were great but there were some things about it that you wanted to improve? Did you take the time to do an analysis of that speaking engagement, making a list of what worked and what didn't work? Did you give out evaluations and review those evaluations, regardless of whether or not the meeting planner had their own feedback forms, looking at what comments your attendees made and why?

Do you speak before your peers so you can get feedback? Or offer to do a complimentary session at a company or public seminar so you can gather some input about what your speaking skills are like now, not last year, five years ago, or even a decade ago? Especially if you're trying out a new topic, or updating a topic you've spoken on before with new material, getting feedback can be the best way to learn, and to improve, since speaking, much like writing, is a skill that needs to be used again and again so it doesn't stagnate.

With speaking, you cannot stay at the same place with your skills or with your topic or even your examples. You either improve on what you are saying or you go backwards. Speakers cannot stand still because the world, and everyone in your audience, is moving forward or backward as well and you've got to keep up with them or, if possible, be ahead of them. Many people go to hear speakers because they are the visionary ones, they are the trailblazers, the forward thinkers, who are leading the way. You are, after all, in the front of the room. You are the speaker and you have been chosen to have this revered position of importance in the room because you do know something, or have wisdom, that others can benefit from.

Secret #12: Develop your own speaking style and brand.

It won't happen overnight but at some point, you need to become distinctively "you" as a speaker. That's when you have moved from speaking on a topic to being a speaker with a style all your own so that no one else could be chosen to imitate you because you are so fresh, so bold, so memorable.

For example, Sam Horn is known for the memorable titles to her communication and people-skills books such as *Take the Bully By the Horns* and *Tongue Fu!*. Or when I heard Larry Winget speak, I initially felt as if he was insulting me and the audience of speakers but by the end of his speech, I realized he was "telling it like it is" (at least like he saw it) and I found his point of view, even if I differed with it, refreshing in its boldness. Those are just two of the hundreds, thousands of top speakers who have developed their own style. That is the last, but the biggest, secret to speaking in public and in a way that you are less likely to fail. Because you are "you" and who is better at being you than you?

Don't try to become or be someone else. Yes, you can observe other speakers, and see what they do that's unique and special, but you want to develop your own style. What is unique about how you, everything from the clothes you wear to the titles of your speeches to the way you go about researching and preparing your presentations, to whether or not you use PowerPoint and, if you do use it, how use it. Your business cards, your letterhead, any imprinted giveaways for your audience. Each and every element of your speech or workshop, and especially your ideas, needs to be your own speaking style. You want to become branded as "you." You are unique. Work with your individuality and let it work for your presentations and your speaking career.

Chapter 6
CULTURAL CONSIDERATIONS WHEN YOU SPEAK

In my book *Grow Global,* I discuss cultural considerations that need to be addressed if you are considering doing business internationally. Those are fundamental protocol issues that will impact on your speaking presentations as well.

Business protocol or strategy concerns for speakers

Here are the fifteen protocol concerns that I discuss in my book, *Grow Global*[1]:

1. Correct Pronunciation and Writing of Someone's Name
2. Proper Greetings and Introductions
3. The Exchange of Business Cards
4. Dining and Eating Customs
5. Punctuality
6. Meeting Concerns: Location
7. Who Will Attend the Meeting?
8. Proper Dress
9. Acceptable Written or Spoken Language
10. Gestures and Body Language
11. Negotiating Styles
12. Topics or Politically Incorrect Issues to Avoid

---

[1] *Grow Global* by Jan Yager, Ph.D. (Stamford, CT: Hannacroix Creek Books, Inc., 2011)

13. Gift Giving and Receiving
14. Holidays and Vacation Time
15. Religious Practices and Related Concerns

Let's look at each of these concerns in the context of public speaking.

#1: Correct pronunciation and writing of someone's name.

If you are going to call on someone in your speech, be careful about how you pronounce his or her name. If you are unsure, apologize in advance, "Please correct me if I get the pronunciation of your name wrong. Mr. So and So?" Of course you only have to say that if it is an unfamiliar or complicated name and you think you're going to get it wrong. You don't have to do it for each and every name you say.

The same is true if someone says his or her name and you want to write it on the board at the front of the room. "Did I spell your name correctly?" is okay to ask, or "Let me know if I got your name down correctly" gives your audience permission to correct you without anyone losing face.

You can say and write your name for your audience as well. If your name has an unusual pronunciation, let your audience know what you prefer or expect so there is less of a chance that someone will say it incorrectly and you will have to publicly correct him or her.

#2: Proper greetings and introductions

Most everyone likes to hear his or her name said so if you are giving a workshop and it is set up classroom style, with chairs and tables where a tent card could be placed, if possible print out a tent card with the name in large letters of each attendee. That will help you to be able to refer to someone by name which will usually make an attendee feel as if his or her presence is appreciated.

When the speaking engagement begins, introduce yourself whether or not you are formally introduced. I like to take the time to go around the room and have everyone share his or her name and one fact about themselves that they want to have known, or one goal for the workshop, or where they work, etc. Just one fact and their name or it would take too long. But it helps to make everyone feel part of the experience.

This practice does take time away from your presentation, however, so factor that into your overall speech preparation.

#3: The exchange of business cards.

The motives for going to a speech range from wanting to learn something to wanting to connect with new people or reconnect with those you already know. Business cards provide a way to gather essential information about those you meet for future reference.

At my website, www.drjanyager.com, I posted a blog, "Is your business card selling you and your business as effectively as it could?" You might find that information useful when you go to create or redo your business card.

In this section, however, I want to address something somewhat different which is the exchange of business cards. One way to encourage the exchange of business cards is to have a product that you raffle off after everyone puts their business card into a receptacle.

You can suggest that attendees use the time before or after your speech to share business cards, or during the break.

And of course make sure you have a business card available so you set an example by giving a card to whomever asks for one.

#4: Dining and eating customs

This will especially apply if you are a before or after lunch or dinner speaker. Some meeting planners, to save time, will even expect you to speak during the meal! This of course can be a challenge as much for you as for the waiters or waitresses. But you need to rise to the occasion and make the situation work for you.

If there are cultural or religious eating taboos or preferences that you need to be aware of, find that out in advance. As the speaker, you are going to be under scrutiny including what you do and don't eat or drink.

As the organizer of a speaking event, if you have any say in what food and beverage will be offered, keep the customs of your potential attendees in mind when you make those decisions. For example, there is an increase in the number of people who want to drink decaf coffee; either have a separate pot of decaf coffee available, in addition to regular, or at least have instant decaf coffee packets, along with hot water to make the decaf and/or to make up tea as well.

#5: Punctuality.

Although it's expected that the speaker will be on time for the event, perhaps even arriving as many as two hours in advance to check on everything, you need to know what is "on time" in a particular culture and take it in stride. Yes, you are the speaker, but you are the guest of whatever company or association has asked you to speak. Especially if you are speaking internationally, you might be in a country where "on time" actually means "within an hour or two."

In addition to the cultural differences or expectations about when you start your speech, find out what the "rules" are for your ending. In the United States, in general, you are expected to end right on time. Ending too early, unless there is a really good reason for it, can look like you're "short changing" the audience. And ending even five or ten minutes late, with some audiences, can paint you as a disorganized or out of control speaker. But in some cultures, and in some corporate cultures even within the U.S., going on longer, especially if you're "going strong" and have a lot to say, might be appreciated as being dedicated and giving the situation "your all."

However, in general, be prepared to start on time, stick to the exact amount of time that you have been allotted, and to end on time.

This is especially true if there are many speakers scheduled throughout a day-long program. In an all-day seminar I recently attended, the morning keynote speaker ran over by as much as half an hour. No one wanted to stop that speaker because he was interesting and also a celebrity. The only downside was that everything else during the day was thrown off. They almost had to reschedule the lunch to take place so late in the day that everyone would be starving but instead they were able to rearrange a couple of the speaking "slots" till after the lunch. It was a good example to me, however, of what can happen when the timing of an agenda is not followed more closely.

#6: Location.

If you have any say in where a speech will be given, let your preferences be known. For many who go to hear a speaker, the venue, or speaking site, can be almost as important as the speaker or the attendees. Will this be at an upscale hotel at the airport so it's convenient to get to, or a more modest hotel in the middle of the city that enables attendees to go to other events or restaurants before or after your speech?

Selecting the town or city for an event can be as key as the topic you speak on. The meeting planner for my first events in Japan, who is now retired, once went to a retreat along with several other members of her cooking class. Where was that cooking retreat? In the South of France, followed by a trip to Paris.

#7: Who will attend the meeting?

If this is a public seminar, your audience will be whomever you market to and who responds, pays, and shows up. If you are being asked to speak by a corporation or company, the meeting attendees will be determined by those who hire you. It could be a companywide meeting, and in that case you will have to speak in a way that your message and information is well-received by a wide range of employees, from the entry level administrative assistant to the senior VP or CEO.

You also need to find out, as much as possible, the concerns of those attending the meeting, and even the protocol in terms of topics that you should or should not bring up.

#8: Proper dress.

As the speaker, what dress is expected of you? For some speakers, their dress becomes as distinctive as a "signature" story is for other speakers.

My colleague Pegine Echevarria is a motivational speaker whose black leather outfit defines her as much as her powerful speeches. Oh, and did I mention that she is a former gang member, that she performs stand-up comedy as a way of lowering her stress level, and she rides a motorcycle?

The black leather outfit would not work for me. I try to wear "business casual" or a suit when I am speaking. But when I traveled to Kolkata, India in July 2010 to speak, my luggage did not arrive right away. It looked as if I was going to buy new clothes to speak in since I only had the jeans I had worn on the plane which was, of course, not an appropriate outfit for speaking.

The meeting planner was kind enough to bring me to a shopping center not too far from the hotel. I was looking at clothes made in India; I certainly would have blended in more if I wore one of those tops and pants. But the meeting planner preferred that I get Western clothes. He did not want me to blend in. He had brought me from America and he was proud that I was a Westerner delivering a speech as part of their all-day conference.

I bought the Western-style clothes and was all set to wear that new outfit when, at midnight, my suitcase arrived so I was able to wear my conservative black suit when I gave my speech the next morning.

#9: Acceptable written or spoken language.

As speakers, we are on display. What we say and do is being listened to carefully. Especially if someone speak to students or children, or to special interest groups who might be offended by certain words or terminology, it is pivotal to watch what is said as well as what is written in printed materials related to your presentation. Even the spelling in a PowerPoint presentation or in your handouts is under scrutiny.

Here's an example: Tina Pennington and Mandy Williams are sisters who co-wrote a self-published book called *What I Learned About Life When My Husband Got Fired!* It led to many speaking engagements and an invitation to develop a financial literacy program for high school seniors, which was adopted as a textbook. That resulted in an invitation to speak before several eighth grade classes.

During the first of those speeches, both sisters used some off-color language which, as Mandy Williams noted, "was totally in keeping with who we are in real life." However, as they found out when they read the evaluations of their speech, some of the students found their language inappropriate. Recognizing their mistake, the sisters wrote a formal letter of apology, which they delivered to the school with a request that it be distributed to the students; they also posted their apology letter at their website, http://www.redandblackbooks.com.

#10: Gestures and body language.

Your own gestures and body language are under scrutiny but you also want to be aware of what the gestures and body language of your audience is telling you. Are they interested? Bored? Involved? Horrified?

At a recent speech that I gave, a woman toward the front of the room caught my eye because whenever I made a key point, she would bob her head up and down. I got to where I knew I was on track if she nodded in agreement.

While it's great that I had confirmation from that one audience member, an over-reliance on one audience member giving me positive feedback could have prevented me from seeing gestures and body language from everyone else, which could have given me additional or even conflicting information.

#11: Negotiating styles.

This refers more to the way contracts for your speaking services are negotiated than your speech itself. Are you dealing with a meeting planner who is used to putting every single detail in writing, or someone who is much "looser" in his or her approach to a speaking engagement and for whom having a more formal, detailed contract is going to be a learning experience for him or her?

#12: Topics or politically incorrect issues to avoid.

This is crucial if you want to start off on the right foot with your audience or even if you want to be asked to speak in the first place. When creating titles for your speeches, or descriptions for your topics, unless you are appealing to a very narrow audience, try to make your language and issues as broad as possible. You can always customize when you go into greater detail once you are more aware of who the audience is going to be.

#13: Gift giving and receiving.

Certain cultures will feel duty-bound to give you a gift as part of the act of doing business together; other cultures will expect to get a gift from you as part of that process as well. Figure out what is ethical and legal in your country, and in whatever country you are going to be speaking in, as well as if there are any dollar guidelines that you should know about. For example, it used to be that giving or receiving a gift that was valued at less than $25 was considered acceptable. But now, in many instances, a gift of any kind, whatever the value, is frowned upon and definitely not allowed because for that company, or government, or situation, a gift equals a bribe.

If you are given a gift, and it is ethical, legal, and acceptable to accept it, be gracious. Send a thank you note, by e-mail or by regular mail. Let the person or association know that you appreciate the gift and that you will cherish it but without going too overboard about it.

If you feel it is appropriate to give a gift, select what you give carefully. Giving something from your home town, or a souvenir from where you live, might be a welcome token of your appreciation.

#14: Holidays and vacation time.

When you propose or accept a speaking engagement, be aware of the holidays or vacation time that might be a factor in your speech. If it is a speech at a company, you might want to make sure it is not the day before a three-day weekend when it is possible some or a majority of your audience has decided to add on an extra vacation day to the weekend and you will have a small audience. Even worse, they are denied that request for an extra day off because you are speaking so you show up and they are all angry and hostile toward you and you don't know why.

#15: Religious practices and related concerns.

Be aware of religious beliefs that might impact on what you say in your speech or even how your presentation goes. For example, if you are doing a workshop with a group that is not allowed to have women and men who are not married to each other associating with one another, you would not want to have a small group activity that requires such behavior or it will be uncomfortable for everyone, especially you.

If there are religious practices that require engaging in prayer at a certain time of day or ending a workshop by a certain hour because of a religious holiday that is starting, be aware of all those concerns so you are as successful a speaker as possible. That goes back to knowing your audience as much as possible.

Chapter 7
THE KEYNOTE

Preparing a keynote address, whether it's six minutes or forty-five, is very similar to preparing a blog of three-hundred words, a magazine article of 1,000 words, or a book of 40,000 words. Yes, length will have its own requirements, but whatever the length of the speech, or the length of the writing, you still need a beginning, a middle, and an end.

The opening to your speech

This is where you want to grab the attention of your audience. If they've been asleep or jittery before you get to the front of the room to speak, this is where you want to get them to sit up and take note so they will listen to the rest of your speech because you have established that you do, indeed, have something to say that will impact on them.

You need to get your audience interested, keep their interest, make your point or points, and end with a flourish.

I took a workshop on giving more effective presentations at an annual meeting of the National Speakers Association (NSA) a few years back. I walked in a few minutes later to the presentation to find Olympic athlete, motivational and keynote speaker Vince Poscente giving his presentation perched on top of a chair; that certainly got my attention and it also stayed in my mind all these years later.

In Chapter 4, I mentioned the trend at NSA to ask their presenters to get to the heart of their presentation within the first 90 seconds, rather than having long introductory comments. What are some of the ways to get that instant attention? You may find any of the following techniques an effective way to get your audience to quickly take notice of you:

- Use a powerful quote.
- Ask a provocative question.
- Tell a joke. (Only do this if you're really good at this and the joke isn't so old that everyone's heard it before. Be careful to pick a joke that won't offend anyone in the audience.)
- Share a dramatic statistic.
- Tell a compelling story
- Give a strong example or a memorable anecdote.
- If you had the audience fill out a survey while waiting to speak and you've been able to tabulate the results, share your findings.
- Show a dramatic audio-visual whether it's a still photograph or a film. (A short documentary providing an overview of her career is how ski racer Bonnie St. John, mentioned in Chapter 5 on speaking secrets, started her presentation that I experienced.)
- Play music.
- Use a memorable prop.

Although this chapter is focused on the more typical keynote address, the forty-five minute presentation, let's not forget that length alone is not the issue. I was recently reminded of this by a news report on CNN that in 1992, a 12-year-old girl, Severn Cullis-Suzuki, gave a six-minute speech when she addressed the delegates in Rio de Janeiro, Brazil on the environment. It was the 1992 U.N. Earth Summit and she became known as "the girl who silenced the world for six minutes."

According to Amy Goodman of www.democracynow.org, the video of that speech has been viewed more than 21 million times on www.youtube.com.

Here's how Severn Cullis-Suzuki began her six-minute keynote back in 1992:

> Hello. I'm Severn Suzuki, speaking for ECO, the Environmental Children's Organization. We're a group of 12- and 13-year-olds trying to make a difference — Vanessa Suttle, Morgan Geisler, Michelle Quigg and me. We've raised all the money to come here ourselves, to come 5,000 miles to tell you adults you must change your ways.
>
> Coming up here today, I have no hidden agenda. I am fighting for my future. Losing my future is not like losing an election or a few points on the stock market. I am here to speak for all generations to come. I am here to speak on behalf of the starving children around the world whose cries go unheard. I am here to speak for the countless animals dying across this planet because they have nowhere left to go.
>
> I am afraid to go out in the sun now because of the holes in our ozone. I am afraid to breathe the air, because I don't know what chemicals are in it…

Reread those openings words. Look at how simple and clear Severn's words are and how she also uses repetition so well. "I am here to speak" and "I am afraid to."

In the very beginning of her speech, she sets the stage for us. She tells it like it is and it is powerful and attention-getting. Twelve and 13-year-olds addressing adults. Raising the money themselves to travel 5,000 miles to tell it like it is.

I am sure no one who was at that Summit, and no one who has viewed that video on www.youtube.com, will ever forget those words, that six-minute keynote address.

Here's an example shared with me by the speaker of how JP Jones, a web designer based in Nashville, Tennessee, opened one of her sessions entitled, "Social Media and You":

So you wanna promote your brand? Drive traffic to your site? Get noticed on the Web? Sounds a little overwhelming, doesn't it? If you are armed with the proper tools and tasks to get the job done, it's simply a matter of being willing to put the time and effort into your venture. When establishing a brand, company, ministry or business in today's marketplace, one of the primary necessities to success is having a successful Web site. Notice I didn't say "having a Web site". The phrasing is "Having a SUCCESSFUL Web site". What's the difference? The social media outlets you use to drive traffic to the site.

Another sample opening to a speech is this one provided by Derrick Hayes, a motivational speaker and author of *1 WORD is All it Takes*:

> First of all I would like to say Good Morning. (The crowd responds)…Good Morning. I know we can give life a better response so this time I want you to respond like you have a bill due, no money to pay it and out of nowhere a check comes to you in the mail.
>
> Good Morning. (The crowd responds with greater energy) Good Morning.
>
> It feels good to be able to share my gift of Derricknyms where I turn names into positive messages. I would like to thank a few people that I met this morning that were extra helpful. Steve that helped me with my bags here is a Derricknym for you. STEVE means Strive To Embrace Victory Everytime. Amy is another nice person that helped me this morning and here is a Derricknym for you, AMY means Always Market Yourself.
>
> I bring you greetings from Georgia where Everyday Is Great In The Peach State.

After your opener, you may want to emphasize to the audience what you are going to offer them over the next forty to forty-five minutes. You may want to hand out an outline, or write it on the flip chart, so your audience has a blueprint for your speech.

The body of your speech

The longest part of your speech is where you focus on the main points you are going to make and you back up each point with examples, statistics, anecdotes, and visual aids, if you have any.

A forty-five minute speech will probably enable you to make three main points, backed up with examples and anecdotes. (I have found that I can usually just cover in a memorable way one main point if I am asked to give a five- to ten-minute presentation in a panel situation or one to two main points for a shorter twenty-minute presentation.)

During the main part of your speech, try, if possible, to keep your audience involved by making your speech interactive. Ask questions of your audience so you will have material to work with right from your audience members. Let's say you're giving a talk on writing. Instead of just sharing about your own experiences getting published, or having writer's block, you could ask the audience, "Let me see by a show of hands if you've ever had writer's block?" If the entire audience holds up their hands you could comment, "So all of you who thought you were the only one experiencing writer's block, you now know how common it is." You might follow up that first question with a related question to elicit an example or anecdote: "Those of you who have experienced writer's block, would you please share what you think caused it, what you were blocking about, who you broke through your block, and how long it took to break through your writer's block?"

Another technique during this main part of your speech to keep it interactive with your audience is to use role playing. Ask for volunteers of one or two audience members to role play, or act out parts in a scenario that you suggest. If it's a controversial topic, you might also be one of the role playing participants.

Another technique you might use is breaking the group up into small groups of four to six and electing one person as the note taker and presenter. Give each group a topic that they explore and then have the presenter share with the entire group what they concluded.

Keep the time allowed for the exercise down to three to five minutes so the entire time allotted to the presentations is seven to ten minutes.

Question and answer session

If your audience expects a Q&A session, make this the third part of your speech. Avoid having the Q&A after your ending because you want to end on a strong note that puts the focus back on you and your speech.

Rather than agree to take all questions, give the Q&A a time period and as you near the end of that time period, e.g., five minutes, let the audience know that you're starting to finish up by saying, "We have time for one more question."

The closing

The first consideration is that you have pre-selected what you will use to conclude your speech. Try to avoid just stopping because your time is up with a comment like, "Oh I see that I'm getting the sign that I have to stop speaking." Instead, mentally note that you have to end your speech but end it in a more powerful way using one of the techniques that you used to start your speech. You can lead into your ending by summarizing what the audience has learned during your speech.

You might also want to conclude by bringing the speech full circle: "When we began our time together today, you probably thought this. We have explored x, y, and z and now you are aware of a, b, and c."

If your presentation is followed by something else that seems like a logical transition, you might want to mention that. You could end with a:

- Call to action
- Quote
- Statistic

- Song
- Brief recap of your key points
- Example
- Anecdote

Here's the ending from Severn Cullis-Suzuki's six-minute speech:

> Do not forget why you're attending these conferences, who you're doing this for: we are your own children. You are deciding what kind of a world we are growing up in. Parents should be able to comfort their children by saying, "Everything's going to be all right," "It's not the end of the world," and "We're doing the best we can." But I don't think you can say that to us anymore. Are we even on your list of priorities? My Dad always says, "You are what you do, not what you say." Well, what you do makes me cry at night. You grown-ups say you love us. But I challenge you, please, make your actions reflect your words. Thank you.

Here is the ending that Derrick Hayes shared with me for reprinting in this book that he used in that speech about Derricknyms:

> A few years ago my ex-wife and the mother of my children said she no longer wanted to be with me. In order to start over I moved from Alabama to Georgia.
>
> Mind you, I had limited money, no job, and no place to stay. A childhood friend said I could sleep on his floor until I could get back on my feet.
>
> I was thinking about how my life had changed and I said *woe*. I looked into the Bible and I saw *woe is me*. Next I looked into the dictionary and it read that *woe* was a trial or tribulation.
>
> This is when I heard a voice say, "Before you leave work or go to sleep tonight, give someone a WOE, a Word Of Encouragement."
>
> I started to see things in words that I had never seen before. In the word *life* is the word *if*, and if you don't try who is to say you will succeed. Life does one thing to you: it takes you through something only to make you do something.

Inside the word *look* is the word *ok*. My mother was dying of cancer and she said that it doesn't matter how things look because everything is going to be all right.

I wrote down the word *arrive* and crossed out the first *r* and placed it at the end of the word. It spelled out A RIVER. When you arrive on time and arrive with a purpose, things in your life will begin to flow just like A RIVER.

You want to leave your audience with something to think about. You want to leave your audience on a high note. You want to end by saying something that is strong and memorable so that in an hour, after they have possibly listened to another speaker, that what you said, the key points you were making, are still in their memory.

Here's another ending to a speech, this one provided by Scott Crabtree whom you might remember from a previous chapter gave up his video game and corporate career to become a full-time speaker on happiness at work:

The bad news is that you listening to me does NOT make you happier in a lasting way. You knowing the science of happiness will NOT make you happier. You have to *think and do* this stuff to be happier. So make a plan. Start small, with a plan you have high confidence in. Share your plan because research shows when you publicly share an intention you are much more likely to follow through.

Remember to be happier at work:

1. 'Flow' to goals
2. Practice positivity
3. Prioritize people

In addition to listening to excellent speeches on a CD, over the Internet or in person, and analyzing during and after those experiences what makes the opening, middle, and end of a particular speech work or fall short, you can also read speeches and consider those examples as well. A wonderful book that will help you to strengthen these skills through a plethora of examples is John Kador's *50 High-Impact Speeches and Remarks*. What he does in this book is take a speech and break it down, starting with the basic details about each speech: the event, the theme, the place, the date, the time, the audience, and the length in minutes and words.

Then the speech is reprinted, on the left, with "talking points" on the right. Kador points out the *who, what, when, where,* and even the *why* of what is in the speech, paragraph by paragraph. For example, the fifteen-minute, 1,380-word speech given by Tom Thompson, telecommunications executive, ("Telecommunications in a Wired World") before approximately 2,000 telecommunication professionals, was filled with stories and just enough statistics to make a point. According to Kador, Thompson delivered a visionary speech which ended with a "stirring closing invoking the metaphor of music and dance" (Kador's commentary). Here are Thompson's actual words:

> I hope we've stirred up your imagination a bit today. Can we hear the first strains of the music of the future? If so, the challenge for all of us is to go and dance the night away…"

The evaluation

If possible, distribute and ask for completed evaluations to be returned after your speech is completed. If you give out the evaluations before your ending, you are actually being evaluated on only 75% of your presentation. You can help the situation along by asking the person who introduces you before you begin your speech to let the audience know that the sequence of events will be just that: an evaluation will be distributed after you've concluded your speech.

As a reward for completing and returning the evaluation, give out the handouts for your talk or an imprinted giveaway that you developed just for this purpose.

After your speech is over

Now that you've collected the evaluations, if you decided to give one out, or you just want to provide something that is a reminder of you and your talk, this is the time to do it. It could be a handout, as noted above, or an imprinted item. Make it something useful and, if possible, something related to your speech, such as a bookmark, if you're an author, or a stress "ball" in the shape of currency, if you're a financial planner; a pen, if you just want to provide something that everyone needs that will help them to remember you and your speech; or perhaps a globe key chain, if you gave a talk on traveling.

Some speakers like to take the time to "meet and greet" those in the audience after the speech is over. They make themselves available to answer questions one-on-one for a certain amount of time, whether it's five or ten minutes or even as long as fifteen minutes to half an hour. Some speakers do not want to interact with the audience after their speech and they head right for the exit and a car that is waiting to whisk them away to their hotel, the airport, another speaking engagement, or they drive themselves home.

Whatever you do at the end of the speech, remember that it is still an extension of your speech. Every word you utter, every gesture, everything you do is still you in the role of speaker. So take what you do or say very seriously and remember that your speaking engagement is still very much on the minds of everyone who just heard you. You don't want to be a leader on the podium, with words that are powerful and memorable, and then when you speak to audience members or the meeting planners afterwards, you use language that is less than flattering, or not well thought out, so that anyone says, "I can't believe that's the same person we just heard speak!"

Asking for testimonials

After your speech, and after you get the evaluations, you might want to ask for a testimonial from the meeting planner, unless of course he or she offers one to you, or sends one, first. Especially if you know the meeting planner thought you were great, don't assume he or she was just saying that and didn't mean it if the testimonial is not forthcoming. They could be busy or away or they just plain forgot. So ask directly without being pushy.

Usually they will write the testimonial themselves and that's the best scenario. If they ask you to write something and they'll review it, if you're comfortable doing that, then go ahead. If you're uncomfortable, try to find something in what they said to you verbally that you remember or something they might even have written to you in an e-mail that you could just send back to them and ask if that could be the testimonial. Often people are unaware that they have already provided a testimonial in a more informal way through an e-mail. (Sometimes they are intimidated by having to writing something in a more formal way.)

Time, timing, and the keynote

I started this chapter with the example of the six-minute keynote by then 12-year-old Severn Cullis-Suzuki that is still viewed on www.youtube.com and remembered today, twenty years later. We looked at the structure of the typical keynote with the average length of forty-five minutes to an hour.

There is another type of keynote that I actually find very powerful and effective. It's the twenty-minute keynote. There are some who might not want to accept providing "just" a twenty-minute keynote "slot" or talk, but it can be a great speech and it can be even more effective than the longer keynote where you run the risk of either repeating yourself because you're making the same key point over and over again or frustrating the audience because you're giving them enough information to try to provoke change but it's not long enough, like a three-hour workshop, during which change is more likely to occur.

There is, of course, no ideal time or dreaded time for a keynote. Every speech, whatever amount of time you are given, has its own challenges. But I caution you against turning down an opportunity to give a fifteen or twenty-minute keynote because you just don't think it's enough time.

There is enough time to make a difference, whether it's in under three-hundred words, like Abraham Lincoln's famous "Gettysburg Address" which begins with the immortal words, "Four score and seven years ago our fathers brought forth on this continent, a new nation, conceived in Liberty, and dedicated to the proposition that all men are created equal."

Make a difference with the words you share and focus on that rather than the length.

There is also discussion about *when* you should give your keynote address. Some prefer the morning, when the audience is bright and alert. Others prefer after lunch, because they are already fed and not as concerned with the break for lunch.

Still others suggest avoiding at all costs the dreaded time slot at the end of the day, when everyone is concerned about getting home, or even at the end of a conference, especially if it's two or more days, when everyone has already checked out of the hotel and they're thinking about how they will get their suitcase and head to the airport before the rush.

If you are given your preference for a time slot for your keynote, that's great. Pick the time slot that seems best for you, your speech, and this particular situation. Think back over the speeches that you have given in the past. When do you tend to be most effective?

Consider your habits and personality: as you a morning or a night person? If you're a night person, perhaps giving the 8 a.m. presentation at the beginning of the day might not be your best choice, if you have one. Instead, you might want a 10 a.m. or a 3 p.m. slot.

But if you are told what time you will be speaking, and there's no negotiation room for changing that time slot, make the most of it. Rather than focusing on whether or not it's a good time "slot," focus on whether or not you are preparing and you will be deliver an excellent, a memorable speech, whenever it is presented. Especially if you or someone else tapes your speech, and puts it at your website or on www.youtube.com, it is a speech forever, regardless of the time of day when you originally delivered it.

Chapter 8
WORKSHOPS, WEBINARS, AND OTHER TYPES OF SPEAKING ENGAGEMENTS

My favorite types of presentations are speaking for five to ten minutes, or offering an all-day seminar. The very short speech gives you a chance to have some key ideas and you "wow" them by being brief and memorable. And the longer day gives you a chance to really make a difference in someone's life by providing hours of information and many opportunities for interacting not just with you but with other attendees at the workshop or seminar.

Training versus speaking

If you're giving a workshop or seminar, whether it's in person or over the Internet (the "webinar") you are usually being asked to share your expertise about a particular skill. You are providing in-depth information on your topic whether in a ninety-minute, three-hour (half-day), all-day, or two-, three-, or five-day format.

The expectation is usually different for a keynote speaker versus a workshop engagement. A workshop puts you more in the trainer mode of speaking. You are expected to be knowledgeable about your topic and to engage the audience in one or more audience participation activities.

If you are the keynoter, the expectations are much higher. You are expected to "wow" them with your high-energy presentation. The pacing has to be right.

Some workshop leaders have a co-leader that they work with throughout the day. Others bring in guest speakers to offer relief from having to speak non-stop for six or eight hours or to provide additional points of view, which makes their workshops or seminars even more appealing.

Have you been to all-day training? I have seen today that the trend is to attend two-, three- and five-day training seminars. As information and knowledge in our world is changing and needs to be shared and updated on a continual basis, participating in a one- to five-day training session is an intensive but time-effective way to make sure individuals can upgrade their skills, and keep their knowledge current. It also offers an opportunity to interact with others who share their interests or, if they work for the same company, but in different parts of the world, to get to know each other and then stay in touch through e-mail or Skype after the seminar is over.

What makes a topic appropriate for a half-day versus an all-day workshop?

Sometimes you don't have a choice about how much time you will devote to a particular topic. You are told by the meeting planner, or the company that either employs you or is hiring you as a speaker, that they want a workshop that is ninety minutes or three hours or six hours long. If that's the case, you will probably agree to do the presentation for whatever length of time is asked of you.

But if you have a say in how long a workshop or seminar should be, here are some considerations about the length of the presentation.

Questions to ask to determine the ideal time for a workshop

- If I've given this speech before, what lengths have I already presented it on?
- What length did I feel most comfortable with?
- If I gave a keynote address, did I find myself afterwards saying, "I have so much more to say. I wish I had a whole day to present on this topic."

- If I presented for an entire day, did I have enough material for a second day?

Once you decide how long the workshop is going to be, preparing for your workshop is like preparing a bunch of keynote addresses that are connected by breaks and recurring themes around which you have decided coordinate your day or days.

All day

Here is a sample all-day schedule for an association conference with multiple speakers:

7:30-8:30 a.m.	Registration/Continental breakfast
8:30-8:45	Opening remarks by president of the organization
8:45-9:30	Speaker #1
9:30-10:15	Speaker #2
10:15-10:30	Break
10:30-11:15	Speaker #3
11:15-12:30	Speaker #4
12:30-1:30	Lunch with lunch speaker
1:30-2:15	Speaker #5
2:15-3	Speaker #6
3-3:15	Break
3:15-4	Speaker #7
4-4:45	Speaker #8
4:45-5	Wrap-up

Sample all-day workshop that you give with you giving all the presentations

7:30-8:30 a.m.	Registration/Continental breakfast
8:30-8:45	Opening remarks by president of the organization

8:45-9:30	Topic #1
9:30-10:15	Topic #2
10:15-10:30	Break
10:30-11:15	Topic #3
11:15-12:30	Topic #4
12:30-1:30	Lunch with lunch speaker
1:30-2:15	Topic #5
2:15-3	Topic #6
3-3:15	Break
3:15-4	Activity
4-4:45	Q&A and Wrap-Up

Sample all-day workshop that you conduct with you giving all but two of the presentations (including two guest speakers)

Note: You can ask your guest speakers to speak for twenty minutes or as long as forty-five minutes to an hour. You might find it easier to get a guest speaker if you ask them to speak for twenty minutes, plus a Q&A (question and answer) session than the longer time frame. If possible, offer your guest speaker, especially if you are not offering an honorarium or the honorarium is quite minimal, to adjust your schedule to accommodate the ideal time slot for your guest speaker.

7:30-8:30 a.m.	Registration/Continental breakfast
8:30-8:45	Opening remarks by president of the organization
8:45-9:30	Topic #1
9:30-10:15	Topic #2
10:15-10:30	Break
10:30-11:15	Guest Speaker #1 *(20-minute presentation followed by 5-10 minute Q&A)*
11:15-12:30	Topic #3
12:30-1:30	Lunch with lunch speaker
1:30-2:15	Topic #4

2:15-3	Guest Speaker #2 *(20-minute presentation followed by 10-15 minute Q&A)*
3-3:15	Break
3:15-4	Activity
4-4:45	Q&A and Wrap-Up

The key point about offering a break-out or concurrent session is that you want to break up each of the longer units into a forty-five minute to one-hour topic.

The skills we discussed in the last chapter, "The Keynote," are not that different for the short and longer workshop situation. If you have a longer time frame to work with, remember that you also have bigger expectations from your attendees.

My best advice about how to prepare a half-day or all-day workshop so it's a positive experience for you and for your attendees? Make every minute count. At the end of the half-day or all-day event, you want your attendees to say, "Wow! That was information-packed!" rather than, "They could have condensed it into an hour and I would have gotten just as much out of it."

As you know, I'm an advocate of doing ice-breakers whatever the length of your presentation. But if you are conducting a workshop, there is definitely an expectation from most attendees that there will be an ice-breaker component to the event.

Ice-breakers are those exercises that allow a group to "open up" and "loosen up" so that the barriers to learning, especially if it is a room full of strangers, can be somewhat reduced so the group feels more comfortable learning together and even contributing by asking or answering questions.

As noted before, ice-breakers are as simple as just going around the room and having everyone share his or her name, or add to that where someone works, or what they want to get out of the workshop, or what their top concern is. Ice-breakers, as the name indicates, usually take place at the beginning of a workshop, with the workshop leader starting the ball rolling by sharing something about himself or herself.

To learn what you personally find effective in running a workshop, try attending some workshops especially on a topic related to what you present on or on something that you are especially eager to learn about. Choose a workshop that has a reputation for delivering on content and in an upbeat and memorable style and see what the organizer or organizers are doing that you could emulate. You can choose the workshop based on the topic, the reputation of the leader, convenience, or preferably all of the above.

Of course you are not looking to lift the ideas from those other workshop leaders but you also don't have to reinvent the wheel if there is a schedule that you could apply to your own topic in terms of when to position the breaks, or if there are ice-breakers that you might find useful to adapt to the workshops you are offering as well. There may be PowerPoint "tips" that are working or even service providers for short film clips that you might add to your presentation, without of course duplicating what you've just seen.

If you have a book that relates to the workshop you are offering, even if you give away, sell, or in some way use the book as part of your presentation, you may still want to have customized handouts or information sheets for each particular workshop. It will help your attendees to feel as if you've gone the extra mile for them and that you're not just rehashing the same old stuff.

Some workshop leaders prefer to have a handout, or even a full-blown workbook that leaves out one or two words in the sentence as a way of encouraging audience participation.

Here's an example from the three-day session on training that I took through the American Society of Training and Development (ASTD). In the section on the 4Ps of training — Purpose, Preparation, Presentation, and Performance — in the handout on the 4Ps under "purpose" you will find this sentence:

"Every action is driven by a _____ or _____ purpose."

(The answers were: "known" or "unknown.")

Or from a handout from one of my time management workshops, on the benefits of handling your time well:

Handling my time well means that I am _____ likely to get to appointments on time.

(Of course the answer is "more.")

Or from a handout from a workshop on friendship:

"Practically every friendship will, at one time or another, have some _____ but that doesn't mean it has to _____."

(Possible answers include: "conflict" in the first fill-in followed by "end" in the second. Other answers might be "betrayal" or "disappointments" in the first instance followed by "lead to more betrayal" or "be put on hold" in the second fill-in.)

Webinars and teleseminars

In 2011, I went from having never given a webinar to offering several within a few months through a variety of corporate, association, and government sponsorships. Although initially I found the thought of it intimidating, when I actually got to do it, the experience fortunately went smoothly, in terms of the technical side of it, and the speaking part of it was unique yet powerful. What makes offering a webinar so amazing is that without leaving your office or home, you can be speaking live with one or hundreds of individuals throughout your city or around the world. And then it is possible to archive that live webinar so that it can be downloaded and listened to again for a certain period of time or forever.

The basic difference between a webinar and a teleseminar is that a webinar uses the Internet as an added component to the presentation. You are able to show your attendees visual materials in support of your presentation. When I offered those webinars, I chose to coordinate the verbal portion with the display of a PowerPoint presentation which was coordinated to my verbal comments.

Even though I don't recommend using PowerPoint as a way of summarizing your talk when you are speaking in public because it distracts the audience from looking at you and making eye contact, when you do a webinar, you are not there in person, so the PowerPoint outline of your talk works very well.

A teleseminar is similar to a webinar in that you and your audience are not in the same place but the teleseminar relies only on a telephone or speaking through the computer, if the teleseminar is done through Skype, but without the visual component with slides like PowerPoint.

What is important to note here is that being unable to physically get to a place is no longer a reason to hold back on sharing the information that you have to offer because you prefer to avoid traveling whether for lifestyle, time, or financial reasons. If you are not already doing webinars or teleseminars, consider adding these ways of speaking to your arsenal of speaking methods.

Participating on a panel

I once asked the agent for a famous etiquette expert if his client would appear with me on a panel. There were going to be hundreds in the audience; it would have been a chance to sell her book or to get media attention for the panel discussion.

Her agent's answer was a resounding "no." He quickly added, in these or similar words, "So-and-so doesn't share the stage with anyone else."

I remember those words loudly and clearly and I have been on enough panels before or after that comment that I can see why he said it.

Fortunately there are ways to make being on a panel a positive experience so it is worth your time and effort. Be careful, however, to factor in to your decision that the nature of the panel experience is that no one gets to speak for very long. Depending upon how many others are on the panel, the audience might even find it hard to remember who you are because there are just so many people up there and, as may often happen, there aren't even tent cards to help the audience to know who's who.

The reasons to agree to be on a panel include: it's in your home town, and you don't have to worry about the time or expense of getting to the event; or you are given a fee, and your airfare and all other expenses are paid for; or it is a prestigious panel of successful people, and you will be associated with that group. You might network with the other panelists to the betterment of your career; or, you might find just being at that event, and on that panel, raises your profile. You might enjoy what you learn from the other panelists; you would not have been exposed to the panel if you were not on the panel because you would not have attended the event.

So deciding whether to participate on a panel, as with all speaking engagements, is to answer that all-important question: Why are you doing it? This is a key question to ask and answer because it will help you to feel less frustrated if the experience fails to move your speaking career forward in the way that delivering an amazing keynote, or a concurrent session that everyone talks about, is likely to do.

In general, however, there is less preparation and pressure if you are on a panel but you are still being presented as a public speaker with opinions worth hearing.

Take your acceptance to be on a panel seriously, just as you would with any speaking engagement. Whether you are paid or it is a free event, whether there are five on the panel or just two, you are giving your word and except for a catastrophe, in the speaking business, your word truly is your bond. The first rule of speaking is to show up at the designated location or, in this electronic world, show up at the Skype live event. (Speaking electronically is not the same thing as being there in person and to do the mixing and mingling that so many like about being on the panel in the first place.)

Here are some dos and don'ts if you do accept being on a panel:

Panel do's

1. Be on time.
2. Be succinct and clear in your answer.
3. Stick to whatever time frame you are given for your reply.
4. Do as much research and preparation as is necessary so you are knowledgeable in the subject matter that you have been asked to speak on or, if you are already an expert, you update your information so the audience does not think what you are sharing is stale.
5. Hang around afterwards and meet the audience members who want to reach out to you. That's probably one of the reasons they came to this event and paid all that money or spent all that time to hear your panel.
6. Try to look as if you're enjoying the experience and hopefully you are.

Panel don'ts

1. Don't monopolize the panel!
2. Avoid always having to have the "last word."
3. Don't badmouth other panelists or colleagues especially those in the room.
4. Watch your language.
5. Even panels get covered by the media. Don't say anything that you don't want to read written up on the front page of the *Times of India*, the *New York Times*, or the most popular website in the world.

Facilitating

Every speaker is probably going to do some facilitating as part of that presentation whether it is a keynote with just a short exercise or activity that you facilitate or a three-hour workshop and you facilitate a twenty-minute activity.

If you are hired to be a facilitator, rather than a speaker, you have to be aware of the differences between facilitating and speaking and make sure you are comfortable with the facilitator role.

A facilitator, unlike a speaker, is not expected to be a content provider or an expert. Instead, it is your job or role to help the group with their meeting.

What are the ground rules for the meeting? When will it start? When will it end? What is the purpose of the meeting? Is there an agenda already in place or will you help the group to create one? Who will be the record keeper and time keeper for the meeting?

If there is a specific task that the group is supposed to be doing, it is your job to make sure that the group is clear about that task.

Another job of the facilitator — and here a professional speaker, if you encourage audience participation in your speeches, would do the same thing — should be watching out for attendees who want to take over the meeting, and stop that from happening, as well as encouraging group members who are shy or silent to more actively participate in the group and in the activity, and to call for a break when one is needed as well as listen and observe about what is going on and to offer feedback to the group.

As the facilitator, you would help to end the meeting by comparing what was achieved to the agenda that had been set up, and discussing what the action plan is as well as any future meetings that need to be decided upon.

You can see that being a facilitator is quite different from being a professional speaker. Facilitators can help move a meeting along but you should be cautious about accepting a facilitator assignment if you have no expertise in this area just because someone asks you because they assume since you are a speaker that you will also be able to facilitate.

But remember that when you are giving a workshop, you may go back and forth between the role of expert and presenter and facilitator as the group carries out activities and exercises that are part of the learning experience.

Toast

The toast should be positive and praiseworthy. If possible write out your thoughts beforehand so you're less likely to share an intimate detail or embarrassing story "on the spot."

If you feel you're not the right person to make the toast, whether it's at an engagement party, wedding, or the retirement party for your best friend, let the organizers know far enough in advance so a replacement can be found.

It is an honor to be asked to give a toast and in some situations, such as a wedding, there is a protocol about who will give it. But if you are not up to the occasion, for a whole host of reasons, it's better to decline politely than embarrass yourself or the person or persons in the spotlight.

If you do accept, make sure you remember that the toast is about the person who is being toasted, not about you or about some political agenda. If your friend is retiring, reflect on what he's accomplished over his years of employment. If you brother is getting married, talk about his good traits as a brother, one or two fond childhood memories that are endearing not embarrassing, and wish the couple well.

No one cares whether you are or see yourself as a professional speaker. You've been asked to speak because of your relationship to the person being toasted and that's what you need to focus on. Don't worry about whether or not a scout for a top speaker bureau is in the audience, judging what you say and how you say it. This is not the right situation for that.

But you still want to be good because it will reflect on the person being toasted so give it your all.

Roast

Today roasts have become all the rage, even being broadcast on TV, like the roast of actor Charlie Sheen. Roasts. You either love 'em or hate 'em and for better or worse, I'm in the last category. I do not want to speak at a roast. I know roasts are tongue-in-cheek and whatever insults are heaved on to the one being roasted aren't supposed to be taken seriously, but I was taught a long time ago, "There are no jokes," and I feel that way when I hear a roast. I cringe at what's being said even if it's followed by "Only kidding."

But if you don't feel that way, and you're asked to speak at a roast, just remember that those who smile in public from your jokes or comments might not still be smiling in private. So consider who the roast is for. Is it for your old friend from high school or your boss? Is it for a co-worker who you know can be very vindictive, or someone you play squash with that you know has a great sense of humor?

And even if the scout for a speaker bureau likely won't be in the audience, if you have plans of competing in that stand-up comedian contest, remember that it's possible there are a lot of smart phones in the audience and it's not impossible that your roast comments and speaking engagement will end up on www.youtube.com. So if anyone is going to do a search of you and you are going to be considered for any kind of speaking engagement, not just a comedic one, be prepared to deal with the consequences of your roast comments for days, months, or even years to come.

If you do participate in the roast, try out your "routine" on people you can trust in advance and see what they think of your jokes. Funny? Witty? Mean-spirited?

And the label of "speaker" or "professional speaker" does follow you wherever you go, just as a writer has to always be concerned with the effectiveness of anything he or she writes.

Commencement address

Some of us dream of being asked back to our alma mater to speak about all we've learned since graduating and to be held up as role models to the new graduates and even throughout the school, nationally, or internationally as a success.

Whether you're asked to speak to the high school graduating class, or college, whether it's your alma mater or just a school that asked you because of your reputation or you knew someone who knew someone, take this role seriously because it is an honor.

You might not get paid, or if you get an honorarium, it might be very small or you're asked to donate it to the charity of your choice. But this is not a gig that has anything to do with money. This is your chance to give back. To influence the next generation. To share what you've learned and, with the benefit of www.youtube.com as well as smart phones, to have your speaking skills showcased for all to see. You might even end up on the evening news, not just in your own city but around the world, so make your ideas powerful and original, and make your words count.

When Steve Jobs, co-founder of Apple, died, the media of course interviewed the author of the new biography of Steve Jobs. Going beyond that, the media also went to the words Jobs shared when he spoke on June 12, 2005 at Stanford University. In that commencement address, the media felt the viewers, who were all in a state of shock over Jobs' death, would find the essence of the man. A man who had dropped out of college. He shared three points in that commencement speech and he ended it by saying, "Stay Hungry. Stay Foolish. Thank you all very much." You can read the entire address at:

http://news.stanford.edu/news/2005/june15/jobs-061505.html

That's the potential power of a well-crafted commencement address. It may actually be the most important speech you ever give.

And if your own child is part of that graduating class and that is one of the reasons that you were asked to speak, you will have that much more pressure on you. But be careful about what, if anything, you share about your child with the other students, faculty, or guests. You don't want to embarrass your child and you also want to remember that this moment, this opportunity, is about what you can give to those students, the staff, faculty, and guests, and not just to your one child.

If you are asked to give a commencement speech, find out what speech length they are looking for and stick to it. There may be other speakers or events that depend on everything running on time. Don't go on and on because you want this amazing opportunity to last as long as possible. Going over the allotted time you are given will backfire.

Finally, ask yourself what you would have wanted to have heard when you were sitting in a similar position. What could someone have told you at your graduation that might have helped you? That would have stayed with you? That might have even changed the course of your life?

Eulogy at a memorial service

The best advice for these types of public speeches are to:

- Speak from the heart
- Keep it short
- Avoid badmouthing the deceased
- While it is okay to share something personal or a little-known fact about the deceased, avoid gossip that would be embarrassing to the deceased or to his or her family, friends, or employer.

In summary

Being known as a professional speaker does come with its responsibilities. It's like a doctor or nurse who would be expected to give immediate aid on a plane or if there was an emergency medical situation at any time or in any place, you may be asked to speak as soon as someone knows that you do it professionally.

Of course it's up to you if you want to speak on the spur of the moment or not. Two situations come to mind where this happened to me.

A woman's group I used to belong to had a Sunday morning luncheon meeting and one of the members was going to address the group but she had a last-minute emergency and they were without a speaker to address the group. The president asked if I would fill in.

I immediately said yes, but instead of just speaking off the top of my head, I sat down, pulled out a sheet of paper, and made an outline for a ten-minute speech on how parents can encourage creativity in their children since I would be addressing a room full of mothers with school-age children.

I gave the talk and it was one of my best.

The other time I was asked to speak out-of-the-blue was when I went to a fundraising dinner organized by a family's relative. I was actually visiting another family member and went to the dinner because I happened to be in town. But when the hostess found out I was at the event, she knew I was an author and that's why she asked me to speak.

Fortunately I had been doing enough work on my speaking skills that I was ready to "jump into action" after taking a few moments to gather my thoughts, make a brief outline of the key points I wanted to make, and to take that opportunity, in just ten or fifteen minutes, to share with the guests.

I guess the part of those experiences, and, if it happens to you, it will strike you as well is that you can't just "wing" it even if someone asks you to speak at the last minute. You have to think long and hard about what you want to say in this precious time that you are being given, no matter the length.

Those who hear you, if it goes well, will think it's effortless and that you can do this without any thought or planning.

Let them think that! You and I know that it is because of all the thought you have put into understanding the role of the professional speaker that enables you to give a memorable talk whether you've been preparing it for a week, a month, a year, or just a few minutes before you get in front of that audience.

You have taken an unspoken pledge to make every word count, to work at making every speaking opportunity that you are offered a powerful and special one. I know you can and will do it because that's what we professional speakers do!

Chapter 9
THE MECHANICS OF SPEAKING

Microphone and audio equipment

I'm not going to spend a whole lot of time in this chapter discussing such technical issues as your microphone or the audio system that you need when you speak before a group of six or more. But what does matter is that you realize this is a consideration that can sabotage an otherwise brilliant speaking engagement because if anyone sitting anywhere in the room, especially in the back rows, can't hear you, it's not going to be a positive experience for them no matter what you say, or how persuasively you say it, because they probably won't even hear you.

Get to your speaking engagement with enough time to check the sound system, at least one hour before, preferably two. You may decide to bring your own microphone along because you have a preference for a lapel mike or a handheld mike. But whether you bring your own or use the one provided by the hotel or meeting facility that you are speaking at, you want to check the sound system to make sure that it is working. And of course, if possible, you want to check it before the audience starts to arrive. There is nothing as unprofessional as technicians, speakers or meeting planners running around right before or after a meeting starts, screaming out, "Testing, testing, testing, one two three," or doing a sound or mike check and having the audio system resonating in everyone's ears because it's not working right.

When you first get asked to speak, find out just what sound system they have available, if you will be able to have a microphone during the event, what kind of microphone, and anything else you need to discuss about the sound part of your talk. Since you are a speaker, this is essential to your speaking engagement just as it would be fundamental for a piano player to make sure there was a piano available for the performance and that the piano had been tuned.

Seating arrangements

Why discuss seating arrangements in a book on the fundamentals of speaking since the focus of this book is how you can be a better speaker? That's because the way you set up your room can make a big difference in how certain speeches are received.

We know from our previous discussion that adults learn best in more informal learning environments. Hence the trend to workshops that take place in the ballroom or meeting room of a hotel with tables of six or eight and with attendees sitting at those tables, rather than in more formal classroom style settings.

But even a classroom style setting will be a better way to have your meeting room arranged if you are giving a workshop that will require your attendees to do a lot of writing and carrying out activities than if they are in a theatre style arrangement where it will be hard to put a pad on your lap and write for any length of time.

If possible, don't leave any of this to chance. Right when you agree to give your speech, find out what arrangements are available and, if you have any say in the matter, let the meeting planner know what seating arrangement will work best for you. Draw a picture if a diagram is not provided.

This will also impact on where the screen should be positioned if you're going to use PowerPoint. If the screens are behind you and you want to see the PowerPoint without turning your back on your audience, you will need to have a teleprompter or a computer that shows you what the audience is seeing, positioned somewhere in the front of the room that enables you to still talk and present while looking at the visual materials.

Here is a picture of me presenting in a concurrent session on how selling a book internationally could help catapult someone's speaking career at a Global Speakers Summit in the Netherlands in April 2011. The classroom set up was fine for this particular presentation because there was minimal writing required of the attendees and the workshop was only an hour. If it was going to last two or more hours, and if having audience participation were pivotal, I might have requested a different set up for the room. It was a small enough group that using a flip chart worked perfectly, allowing for the audience participation and immediacy of feedback that I had wanted for this particular talk.

PowerPoint, flip charts, other audio-visual aids, handouts, and props

The essence of an excellent speech comes down to what the speaker has to say, and how he or she says it, but there are fortunately tools that can help you in the delivery of your message. It does not have to be just you and your words and the audience. There are all kinds of visual aids, like PowerPoint, or an old-fashioned but still highly effective flip chart, especially in smaller group settings of six to fifteen people.

In this chapter we'll look at some of those tools that can help you to be more effective as a speaker.

PowerPoint

PowerPoint is a software program developed by Microsoft that has become widely used internationally as a way to create presentations that are developed on your computer and then shown during your actual presentation through a computer (or a flash drive) projected on to a screen in the front of the room.

There is a Mac version of PowerPoint that you can use on an Apple Mac computer, or you can also use the Mac Keynote software to create your presentation instead.

I am not going to compete in this chapter with the manuals or books that are available about how to do a PowerPoint presentation. Instead, the purpose of this chapter is for those who are using PowerPoint to consider whether it is helping or hurting their presentations, and for those who never use it, to consider whether there are situations when it might be useful.

The first consideration is how you will use the PowerPoint tool. Will it be a way to keep you on track by outlining your main points and sharing these in your PowerPoint display? Or will you use PowerPoint the way Michael Landrum, a PowerPoint coach, recommended in a workshop on PowerPoint: to accent or emphasize the points that you're making, to insert photographs or illustrations and just a word or two to make a point, and to enhance your presentation, rather than highlight or summarize it.

Here, excerpted, with permission, from Mike Landrum's website in his excellent article, "Personalizing PowerPoint," are some suggestions that should help any speaker who wishes to use this amazing technology so it improves rather than hurts your presentation[1]:

When PowerPoint becomes a sort of Teleprompter, projected on a screen and then read aloud to an audience it can turn a roomful of MBA's into a lynch mob. How to fix this problem? Here are seven suggestions:

1. Turn the dang thing off: Push the 'B' key at regular intervals, let the screen go blank and step forward to address the audience personally. Even better, insert a "buffer" slide – blank, between each of your few important illustrative slides. Go to your paper notes instead. Establish contact. Tell them a story. Notice as you do, the sigh of relief that will issue from your listeners.

2. Trim the content: Three to five strong, valid points are all most audiences are capable of absorbing in one sitting. Present the crucial information and cut everything else. Put the cuttings in a handout, white paper or article, but resist the impulse to inflict every last iota of information on your audience.

3. Simplify the language: Get rid of jargon. Written language tends to use complex, compound words – spoken conversation is more simple and direct – and much easier to understand. Consider these events 'talks' rather than 'articles.' Use repetition and various ways of illustrating the same point.

4. Give them pictures: Find graphic ways to express the essential points you need to make. Graphs, drawings, diagrams, photos, video clips, etc., are visual expressions that work well projected onto a screen. Words are abstract intellectual expressions that work best on paper and spoken aloud.

5. Take the time to PRACTICE: Lack of time is the most frequent excuse for this whole sorry pattern. The exec is too busy, so she has her assistant create some slides and then all she has to do is read

---

[1] Excerpted and reprinted, with permission, from "Personalizing PowerPoint," posted at http://www.coachmike.com/personalppt.shtml

them off. And if she makes time in her schedule what does she do with it? She spends it fiddling with the slides, making them twinkle, instead of practicing her delivery.

6. Make it flexible: Give yourself the option of showing a wide variety of graphics if the need arises. Make your presentation capable of answering the audience's questions. Have an assistant who can switch to any of your slides on request. This lets you jump over un-needed material and adjust to the listener's needs.

7. One input at a time: Let the audience either read the text slide or listen to your speech, but don't ask them to do both at once. If it's a graphic, give them a moment to absorb it before you begin explaining. As with comedy, PowerPoint presenting requires a good sense of timing.

The plain fact is that PowerPoint cannot create rapport. It's a strictly passive form of communication. There is no closing of the loop, no feedback possible; it does not respond well to the immediate concerns of the humans in the audience. It is indifferent and unrelenting. That is why audiences feel so overwhelmed and helpless under a PowerPoint barrage. There is no way to affect the thing as it is normally used these days.

Flip chart

I still enjoy using a flip chart, with brightly colored markers, especially if I'm using it with an audience that is between six and fifteen people and we are sitting in a room that enables everyone throughout the room to see the chart at the front of the room.

Unlike the PowerPoint presentation, which tends to be created well in advance of the speech or workshop, the flip chart, when I use it, is a spontaneous way to emphasize a point that I'm making or write down contributions from the audience if there is an audience participation activity.

If you do use a flip chart, make sure you write in a big and bold way. If you aren't comfortable printing and your long hand writing is hard to decipher, you can ask one of the audience members to be the secretary for the presentation, writing down what you suggest on the flip chart.

Other audio-visual aids

As an extension of PowerPoint, or as a way of engaging your audience, consider showing a short movie. This can be a very effective way of making your point. It can be a movie that you created just for this presentation or it can be a clip from a movie that makes a point for you better than just words. You can also rent or buy movies that will address the theme that you are dealing with and as long as you don't select a movie that you think has been shown too many times so that the audience will be bored, adding a visual aid to your presentation will impress the audience because it makes you look like you care enough to go to the trouble to have additional materials. But be careful that what you say is still powerful and memorable or you run the risk of having your audio visual materials getting an "A" in your evaluations and your speech is seen as far less impressive.

Handouts

I went to a presentation by speaker Ed Peters and he made the point that no one was in need of a "handout" so why not call it an "informational sheet"? It's a great point and over the years, I do try to say "informational sheet" instead of "handout" but I usually go back to the term "handout" because that's what everyone understands and knows!

Whatever you call it, the purpose is the same: to give attendees even one sheet at the beginning of the presentation, with the agenda that they will follow or to give it to them at the end, with a summary of the presentation as well as some suggested resources. You can also use handouts in the middle of your presentation especially if you have activities that you want your attendees to do and you prefer to give them the sheets to work on at the right moment rather than have the materials distributed in advance and running the risk that they'll be reading the materials — handouts — rather than listening to you.

In that same memorable talk that Ed Peters gave all those many years ago, he pointed out the benefits of adding color to your handouts. At that time, using a color printer was a lot more costly than it has become now so it was a radical idea that a handout should have even spot color rather than just black and white. But today, more than ever, with ink jet and even color laser printers so much faster and even more affordable, it makes sense to have information sheets/handouts that are visually appealing as well as well-written and useful.

The advantage to you as a speaker in giving out a handout is that you get another opportunity to influence your audience, and to reinforce what you shared with them. You also can have your contact information on the sheet so there is a greater possibility of follow-up as well as ongoing connection with your audience.

Props

I'm not suggesting that you become a magician or that you have to have a bag of tricks when you speak. But having the well-timed and well-chosen prop can turn an okay speech into a magical and more memorable experience.

If you are going to use a prop, make sure you practice so that you are comfortable doing it. It needs to seem effortless and seamless or it will backfire because you will appear awkward and uncomfortable to your audience.

I was doing a time management presentation once and I had obtained a magic wand. I got to the point in my presentation when I said something like, "Wouldn't it be nice if you could change overnight, just like that?" and I took out the magic wand and tapped it at the right time and in the right way. The effect was exactly what I had hoped it would be and it was a gesture and a prop that reinforced the key point I was making.

What topics are you speaking on? If you do not already use props, brainstorm at least three props for each speech that you might use.

Chapter 10
HOW TO HANDLE TWELVE TOP CHALLENGES YOU MAY FACE AS A SPEAKER

There are, of course, more than twelve possible challenging situations that you will have to deal with as a speaker but the ones that I singled out to discuss below are some of the most common ones that you need to learn how to deal with.

Situation #1: You are afraid to speak.

Although this has been dealt with at other points in this book, the topic is worth emphasizing.

What causes a fear of speaking? Everyone who has this experience, whether it is just once, or right before you're going to speak in public for the first time, or it happens every time you speak, will lead to a different answer to that question. But the reasons you get stage fright probably fall into several key categories:

1. You feel insecure about your speaking skills.
2. You feel like you are unprepared for this particular topic or speech.
3. You have never been asked to speak publicly before so you don't know what to expect.
4. The last time you spoke, it was a disaster.
5. New situations make you afraid and speaking presents you with a new situation.

Let's look at how you can handle each of these reasons so that you can overcome your fear of speaking and do an excellent job and maybe even learn to enjoy speaking!

You feel insecure about your speaking skills

Join your local Toastmasters International and attend their weekly meetings. Get more experience speaking in front of groups and build your self-confidence that way. If you prefer to do it on your own, ask family members or friends if you can speak for them, practicing your speech. If you have no other options, at least speak before a mirror or for yourself. I saw a very impressive presentation projected to the room full of several hundred via Skype when I was at an international speaking summit in the Netherlands two years ago which emphasized how something happens to the brain when it hears *out loud* what you are going to say. Practice by speaking, not just by going over your notes.

Practicing in that way could help you to become more confident and to overcome your fear of speaking.

You feel like you are unprepared for this particular topic or speech

If you feel unprepared, you probably are. So do more preparation. If necessary, write out your speech. Some of my best speeches I wrote out in advance. I then created an outline and I used the outline to present, not the written out version. In a couple of instances, I even published the written out version as an article or used it as the basis of a book. But the act of writing out what I was planning to say helped me to become the master of that speech and it built my confidence so I was much less afraid in front of the audience.

Research your topic. Give yourself ample time to prepare and practice for your speech. It goes without saying but I'll say it anyway: Don't prepare only the night before. Yes, it's okay to practice again the night before but you should have started preparing for this speech days, weeks, and possibly even months in advance. In general, the more prepared you are, the less afraid you will be.

You have never been asked to speak publicly before so you don't know what to expect

Everyone has to start somewhere. I had already spoken before many audiences in the United Kingdom on my author tour, and I had taken public speaking in college, but none of those speeches were for a fee. When I was asked to speak for a fee, and it was a nice fee because the speaker I was replacing was kind enough to ask them to offer me the fee that he would have gotten, I was frozen and afraid, as if I had never spoken before. My boyfriend at the time was an actor so I asked him if he would work with me on my preparation for that speech. We worked on it and I rehearsed and rehearsed and it went really well. It proved to me the value of working with a coach whether it's once or on an ongoing basis especially if this is your first public speech or you feel like it is.

Here's what business coach Mark Raciappa shared with me in a communication what he learned from the first speech he gave when he was sixteen, a lesson about speaking that has stayed with him ever since:

> When I was 16 years old, a junior in high school, my teacher/sponsor in National Honor Society encouraged me to run for State President of the organization (in Florida).
>
> I had never run for any "elected" office before and consented reluctantly. My teacher, parents, and local peers promised support and off we went to the State convention. I was running against two other challengers and we spent three days meeting, greeting, shaking hands, etc. The culmination of the event was a speech in front of the whole assembly (approximately 500 of my peers from all over the state). I had written, re-written, and refined my speech over the previous weeks but had never addressed a crowd this large. When my turn came and I stepped onto the platform, I was

immediately overwhelmed by the magnitude of the crowd and the bright lights in my eyes.

The room quieted after my introduction and I started to speak, reading my carefully crafted speech. My voice started to crack, my hands holding the paper started to shake, and I knew I was "going down in flames". For some unknown reason (divine intervention?), I laid the paper down, held my head up, and simply talked to those folks for the next five minutes, articulating points I had practiced for weeks.

I got through the speech and finished strongly. The lessons that I learned that day have served me ever since. I prepare, practice, and most importantly, make only bullet-pointed notes so that I can make eye contact with my audience and connect with them. I learned that speaking "from the heart" about topics for which I'm passionate is the best approach for me.

The last time you spoke, it was a disaster

You're suffering from PTSD — post traumatic stress disorder — only in this case you're re-living the horrible speaking experience rather than being in a war or having a heart attack. The impact on you can be just as debilitating, however. There are, fortunately, psychologists, psychiatrists, social workers, therapists, or coaches who specialize in helping someone to overcome PTSD.

Okay, remember that not all speeches will be brilliant, memorable, and fabulous. So you had a "bad" speech. Face it. Deal with it. Try to analyze *why* it didn't go well. Is there anything from the experience that can help you to do better next time?

Try to substitute a positive speech memory for this traumatic one. Visualize yourself speaking and it going well. If you got a fabulous testimonial after a speech, reread it. Print it out. Post it on your wall. Reread it and gain strength from it. Try to remember all the times your speaking engagements went well and the few times it was a disaster. If the positive times outweigh the negative ones, that's great. You're going in the right direction even if the last time you spoke it didn't go so well. By the law of averages, if most of the time your speeches go well, this next time is more likely to be a positive than a negative experience.

New situations make you afraid and speaking presents you with a new situation

Yes, speaking before a new group and on a new topic, or even on the same topic but to a new group, can bring out the fear of the unknown. But consider when the unknown can be exciting and exhilarating and not necessarily something to be feared.

Think back to the first day of school when you were younger. You were probably afraid but soon the fear was replaced with familiarity and a positive experience.

The more you speak, and the more you have positive speaking experiences, the more you will be comfortable speaking and less afraid of the experience.

Dwell on the benefits of speaking that make the fear and the dread worth it: getting to share your ideas with others; getting to be part of new situations and even new places; meeting new people; being part of something cutting edge and exciting; expanding your SOI (sphere of influence); learning about fresh ideas, customs, and cultures.

Here are some of the top ways to overcome your stage fright:

1. Dwell on the times it went well for you in the past and on the fact that you wouldn't have been asked to speak if someone didn't think you were capable of doing it.
2. Do deep breathing.
3. The late speaker and head of her own speaker bureau, Dotti Walters, used mental visualization to get over her stage fright. She would visualize herself tucking her children into bed with a soft pink blanket that her family called their comforter. "I filled the whole auditorium with the 'comforter' in my mind,'" Walters writes in *Speak and Grow Rich*.
4. Practice so you'll have more confidence.

5. In *Speak with Confidence*, Dianna Booher writes, "The secret to a great presentation is performing despite the nervousness — in fact, making your jitters work for you. Imagine the tension and extra adrenalin pumping through you as catalysts to a great performance."

6. Do exercises.

7. Remind yourself that even some of the greatest actors and musicians admit that they get stage fright before they perform but they push through the fear and get out there and perform anyway.

Situation #2: Someone walks out.

When I do time management workshops, I will say, "Imagine the worst thing that can happen to you and now imagine yourself coping with it."

In the world of public speaking, having one or more people walk out on your speech is probably one of the biggest fears someone could have about public speaking.

What if that happened? Is it possible to survive something like that?

If you speak to a large audience, sooner or later, someone may walk out. Don't take this personally because chances are it has nothing to do with you. He or she may have to use the bathroom, or just received a text they need to react to. They may even leave because what you're talking about isn't something they want or need to hear. This still has nothing to do with you. So ignore them, let them go, and keep talking to those who have remained to hear your words of wisdom. (It's very important to ignore them and not draw attention to those who are leaving and especially avoid "attacking" those who are walking out. If you make the person walking out feel embarrassed or self-conscious because you're drawing attention to their departure, the audience may turn on you, siding with the person whom you just attacked. The rest of your presentation might then be to a hostile, angry group and you certainly don't want that!)

Situation #3: You get booed.

This has not happened to me and hopefully it never will, but it could happen. Just recently, I read online and in the newspaper that it happened to the President of the United States, Barack Obama, when he was giving a speech: he was booed for inviting Vernon Davis, a San Francisco 49ers football player, to join the Chicago Bears, another team.

Upon further research, I learned that Michelle Obama, the First Lady, reportedly got booed by school children when she gave a speech about having healthier lunches at a school in Virginia in January 2012.

If the President and First Lady Obama can get booed and they get through it, why not you?

Like most "mishaps" or unpleasant situations related to speaking, it's best to figure out *why* it's happening (or afterwards, when you reflect on your speech, and analyze what worked and didn't work about it, why it happened). In the case of booing, try to determine whether:

1. Something you said was controversial.
2. Something you said offended one or more people in the audience.
3. You mentioned a name, place, or event that has a negative connotation to it.
4. The person booing has a reputation for doing that to all speakers.
5. Some other reason???

If the reason is #3, and you will be speaking to a similar audience soon or in the future, try to avoid mentioning those names, events, or places that instantly conjure up negative feelings so that booing is more likely. For example, if you're speaking in Delhi and you say, "The best city in India, Mumbai," you are much more likely to be booed than if you avoid making a statement like that or you say something like, "There is controversy over which city is the best in India."

If the reason is #4, you can try, in the future, to keep that individual out of your speeches, if that's a possibility.

If the reason is #5, you may have to probe further to figure this out, if you are to learn from the experience.

Of course if the statement you make in your speech is pivotal to your speech, and you know that the statement is controversial and likely to inspire heckling or booes, you may decide to make that statement anyway. Just don't take the booing personally. It's something that "comes with the territory" as they say or, if you're a speaker.

If you decide that you can't take the possibility of being booed occasionally, you might have to consider if you have the stamina for this challenging career.

Situation #4: Someone keeps interrupting you.

If there is one person who keeps interrupting you, you have to be careful if you do ask that person to hold his or her questions till the end of the presentation. There is always a chance that the audience may side with the person who is doing the interrupting. So be kind and gentle when you ask this person, politely, to please try to hold his or her questions till the end because the interruptions are making it hard for you to keep your train of thought.

If you're good with humor and, once again, you can do it in a way that is not seen as you turning on this audience member, you could ask if this person who is interrupting would like to take the podium and take over for you? He or she will hopefully get the hint that their constant interruptions have become a nuisance.

If the rest of your audience is okay with the interruptions and it's just you who's annoyed, consider taking it in stride. Answer the person's questions, or ask him or her to ask the questions at the end, and chalk it up to something that happens from time to time that you have to deal with. The key is not to lose your cool or to verbally attack the interrupter because that will definitely backfire and you will be seen as aggressive and insensitive.

A situation related to learning to deal with the heckler is how you react to someone who yawns, especially if he or she is sitting in the front row, it's done in an obvious way, and you see it. Once again, don't take it personally! This person just might have a new baby at home and she hasn't gotten more than three hours of sleep in the last two weeks, or some other reason. Don't automatically assume it's you, and get defensive. If you've had this happen before, and you're good with humor, and you know it will work, and not backfire, you can handle it with humor. But usually it's best to say nothing and just keep going.

That's why a lot of speakers build audience participation into their program, however short or long the program. It's another version of what teachers used to do in the old days: "Now students, let's all rise and stretch." It's a way of getting the audience to stay awake. And also check if the room is too hot. That can cause people to get sleepy especially if it's late in the afternoon and everyone's been at it since 8 a.m.

Situation #5: Your computer (PowerPoint) won't work.

Who hasn't had this happen?

Know that this is a much more common situation than you might think and, because of that, prepare for it by having a hard copy print out of your presentation, just in case.

If your PowerPoint presentation was going to include embedded images and video, make sure you have alternatives that you can use to fill up that time, or to make that point, if you can't access your PowerPoint presentation on the computer. For example, you can show a picture at the front of the room of something you were planning to flash onto the screen. If the image won't be large enough to be seen, show the picture but make sure you go out of your way to describe it in detail so those who cannot see what you are showing at the front of the room can imagine it in their minds.

If you can't show the videos that you had planned to show because your PowerPoint won't work, summarize what the videos were going to be. If it was going to be an enactment or reenactment, see if one or more of the audience members might be willing to act out the scenarios that you tell them about.

Try not to get overwhelmed, baffled, and too upset when or if this happens. Most everyone has done presentations without PowerPoint for a variety of reasons ranging from it wasn't invented or available yet to you forgot your flash drive or the computer malfunctioned. So just go back to doing the presentation as you would have done it before you used PowerPoint, making sure you are as cohesive, interesting, and in control as you would have been if the PowerPoint had functioned.

If you feel comfortable making the offer, you can tell your audience that you will post the PowerPoint at your website and they will be able to download it for a certain period of time so they won't miss out on anything that would have been in the PowerPoint if the computer hadn't malfunctioned.

This is exactly what happened to website designer Jann Mirchandani of Westchester County, New York. But see how she turned the situation around in this speaking story that she shared with me in an e-mail:

> Mine started out as a horror story but ended up being one of the best presentations I've done. I was doing a half-day workshop on online marketing to a group of about 30 or so women business owners. I had rehearsed my presentation and had my slides ready to go. I even had everything backed up on a thumb drive just in case... Because I had my backup plan in place, and I was trying to be green, I didn't print any hard copies.
>
> The day of the workshop I got there early, booted up the laptop and everything was cooking on high, right up until my laptop tried to install some updates and wouldn't reboot!
>
> I was beginning to panic a bit to be honest as people started rolling in and I had NOTHING to refer to and I was there for three hours!
>
> But I set side my planned presentation and decided that we would have a marathon Q&A session. I was introduced, I got up there and gave everyone the game plan.

I went over some of the high level topics I wanted to cover and just let the audience share their experiences and ask their questions about how to handle those situations.

It ended up being an extremely productive session. I couldn't even get out after because people kept coming up to me to thank me and ask more questions!

Situation #6: The audience doesn't want to hear the prepared topic.

In this situation, you are speaking about what everyone agreed you would address, but for a whole host of reasons, it is clear that your audience does not want to hear what you're talking about.

First of all, be sure that your perception about the situation is an accurate one. Before you jump to the conclusion that your audience would prefer to hear a different talk, try to figure out if your "instinct" or your interpretation of their body language is accurate by saying something like, "I'm getting a sense that you're not all that interested in what I was going to talk to you about today. Am I reading your cues correctly?"

See what kind of responses you get. If a couple chime in, "Yes, that's exactly right," follow up by asking, "Why?" Try to find out what's going on before you automatically consider switching to a different topic.

I remember years ago I was supposed to give a presentation on time management to the employees at a media company based in San Francisco. I didn't stop my presentation even though there were many in the audience who were distracted and distant. I wasn't as seasoned a speaker then and I didn't follow-up on the information I was getting from the audience to ask them what was going on.

If I had asked them, instead of sticking to the pre-planned agenda despite the uncomfortable atmosphere, I would have learned before the end of the workshop, rather than afterwards when I couldn't do anything about it, that it had just been announced that morning that the company was going to be sold. So instead of anyone caring about how they managed their time, they were concerned about whether or not they would have a job when the changeover occurred.

If I had learned that that was what was going on, in a non-threatening way, I could have worked in the theme of change in my presentation and how there are things we can control and things outside of our control and how dealing with change is part of time management. If some or all of the attendees had felt comfortable exploring the situation they were going through, without turning it into a therapy session, it might have been an opportunity for them to share about the anxiety they were feeling. Or if that was deemed too threatening and direct a way to deal with it, we could have at least explored it in the more general way.

So if your audience is telling you, or you're reading their non-verbal body language and in that way they're indirectly telling you, that they are bored, angry, or disinterested in the topic you are presenting about, find out why and, if you agree that you should switch to another topic, do it. You are there to serve your audience and, by serving your audience, and serving them well, you will also be pleasing the meeting planner who hired you. (Or, if it's an unpaid speaking engagement, you still want your audience to be pleased because time is still money so you don't want to waste your audience's time and if you do a superb job, unpaid speaking gigs can lead to paid ones.)

So have the outline to another speech available to you if you need to switch to another topic. If that's not possible, turn the speaking engagement into a discussion group. Sometimes your audience attendees can teach each other even more than you can share with them. In that way, you become more of a facilitator than a speaker. (Look back at the suggestions for how to be an effective facilitator from Chapter 8, "Workshops, Webinars, and Other Types of Speaking Engagements.")

Situation #7: You forget what you were about to say or you can't remember a fact.

Here's how the *Telegraph* of the UK described what happened to then-presidential candidate Rick Perry when, on November 9th, 2011, in a presidential debate he forgot what he was about to say:

"Governor Rick Perry of Texas suffered one of the worst stumbles in American presidential debate history when he spent nearly a minute trying and failing to remember the name of a government department he had vowed to abolish."

Governor Rick Perry's memory lapse was one of the most dramatic instances of how excruciating it is for those in the audience as well as the speaker when this situation does occur.

When this happens, and it is bound to happen at some time, it can feel like the most embarrassing situation in the world. It probably doesn't help to remind yourself that it happens to the best professionals in the world, at least every once in a while. (Okay, maybe you're one of those rare people it's never happened to. Congratulations! But what if it does happen to you?)

Here are some suggestions for dealing with this situation:

1. If at all possible, avoid panicking. Panicking will just make the situation worse.

2. Do you have an outline of your speech? Whether it's your PowerPoint presentation, or your notes, if you do have an outline, refer to it. See if there's something in that outline that can help you get back on track.

3. If you still need help, admit to the audience that you've forgotten what you were about to say. "I've forgotten what I was about to say. Bear with me a moment." Or "Senior moment. Let me figure out what I was going to say." Give yourself a moment to figure it out.

4. If that time doesn't help you to get back on track and you still need help, say, "Now what did I just say?" That might help you to remember what you were going to say next.

5. If you know this might happen to you either because it has happened before or you fear it might happen, have available to you notes on topics or issues that you can switch to discussing so you keep going forward in your presentation rather than focusing on your memory lapse. Say "Moving

right along" or use another transitional phrase to help you keep going.

Situation #8: The person that preceded you covered your topic.

Here are two extreme ways of handling this situation. The first way is based on what I observed at a recent media conference that I attended: someone got up to speak and he told us that a previous speaker had covered all the points he planned to make so he would make his speech very short.

In a way, he had definitely handled the situation. I think you probably agree that this was preferable to repeating the same points and boring the audience.

But did he make the most of his time on the platform? He was there for less than a minute. He was accepting an award, which is of course a different kind of speech than if he was delivering a formal keynote address, but he definitely did not make use of this golden opportunity to influence his peers.

Here's a different way of handling this situation. This second way is my own example. Several years ago, I was asked to be a keynote speaker about work relationships at a conference for military librarians being held in Las Vegas. I was going to be speaking on the last day of a five-day conference and one of the speakers during the week was going to be speaking on a topic that was similar to mine. I was so afraid that I would end up repeating the same points that the previous speaker had made, I arrived a few days early for the conference, went to the entire conference, including that other speaker's presentation, and gave my speech, adjusting it somewhat just so I wouldn't repeat the same points as the previous speaker.

That is an extreme way to handle this situation! Yes, I did end up avoiding the repetition of themes from previous speakers, but I was also away from home for five days instead of two, and I still only got paid for delivering the one speech and not for attending a five-day conference!

If you know someone has been asked to speak on a similar topic, if you can attend that speech without too much effort in terms of time and money, do it. There's nothing as powerful as hearing, first-hand, what your audience will also have heard.

But if that's not possible, see if you can at least get a summary of the key points that the previous speaker made. Get those points either from the meeting planner who asked you to speak or even, after the event, from the speaker himself or herself. (You should wait till after their presentation or they may think you're trying to upstage them or they might even feel self-conscious because they might change what they say at the last minute.)

If the other speaker is right before you, which is what happened in the case of the media conference award winner that I recently observed, you won't have that luxury of time to revise your preparation. But you can still use what the previous speaker said to your advantage. Summarize for the audience the points that your colleague made, the points that you were also going to make, as a way of emphasizing what those points are rather than assuming the audience remembered what the previous speaker said.

Then, add your own special wisdom and examples to those points so that you freshen-up each one. You are not boring your audience by repeating the same things, but you're taking the same ideas and adding your own unique "take" on those concepts.

Finally, do a completely different speech than anything you prepared. There are so many speeches you could give at any one moment. Have outlines for a couple on you, just in case. If necessary, make something up on the spur of the moment. but find a way to create an outline that you will follow, even if you only have a short time to prepare and you have to write your outline or notes down on a paper napkin at the table, or on your smart phone. If possible, practice, even if you have to go into the nearby bathroom or an empty room nearby, to go over your opening and your conclusion, and as much in-between as possible.

To create this last minute speech, you can use what happened in that day's news. If you are speaking at a hotel, there is often a selection of local, national, and even international newspapers that you can buy and use. Or you can go online, if you have computer access, and find information that you want to put in your speech so you go in a different direction than the previous speaker.

Ask your audience for their opinions. Provide opinions, yourself.

You could actually turn this situation where you risked being repetitive and derivative into you being stimulating, spontaneous, extemporaneous, and energized as a speaker.

Situation #9: You run out of things to say.

You can help to avoid this happening by always having some extra material that you put into your presentation "just in case." This could be additional examples for each of the key points that you made or it could be articles that you might read or even a visual aid that you might show such as a short video if you're using a computer.

Another way of dealing with this, if you don't think it will backfire and you'll be judged in a negative light, is to end your speech early, let's say up to fifteen minutes ahead of time, rather than being seen as someone who is "padding" your presentation.

How about a question and answer session, if you didn't have one already?

What about doing an "end of the day" ice-breaker? Have those in the audience turn to someone they don't know and share about what is the part of the presentation that most resonated with them. They could then report back to the entire group. That should take five to fifteen minutes.

You could have members of the audience share their expertise related to the topic that you presented on so the time left is used wisely.

Situation #10: You're out of time with more to say.

This is the opposite of Situation #9 where you said what you planned to say and you still have time. If you still have things to say and the allotted time is up, you could see if everyone is able to stay another five or ten minutes as long as this won't backfire and get you labeled by the audience or the meeting planner as someone who is unable to speak within the agreed upon guidelines.

You can offer to post the comments you did not have time to say at your website so that attendees could view the information there, if you feel the information is important enough that you need to share it.

If you see your time is ending, if you had another five or ten minutes of material that you did not get to go through, you could summarize the key points in thirty to sixty seconds so at least you get to share your main ideas.

If this happens to you often, make sure you try harder to plan better so that you pace yourself and your speeches or workshops so you end when you are supposed to end and you cover all the important material you planned to cover.

Situation #11: You don't feel like speaking.

Professional speakers have to speak because they have made a commitment to speak whether it is for a fee or for free. The minute you accept a speaking engagement, you are giving your word. A lot may depend on you speaking. The announcement about your speaking engagement may go into a community newspaper or online website, if it's a public event, days, weeks, or even months in advance of the event. Your reputation, and the reputation of the association, library, bookstore, or company that has asked you to speak, is now tied to that event.

Barring illness, poor weather, or some other extenuating circumstance that makes it impossible for you to speak, you should speak whether you feel like it or not. If you cannot speak because of some unforeseen last-minute circumstance, you can ask if you should provide a substitute speaker. This may not be necessary but it will certainly be appreciated if it is a welcomed offer.

If it is a paid speaking engagement, check your contract on what you promised to do if you cannot speak for whatever reason. Will you pay back the money? Will you find a replacement speaker?

Practically every speaker has times when he or she would prefer not to speak whether it's because they're not in the mood or there's something else going on in their professional or personal life that's a distraction from the speaking engagement. If the speech is in another community or another country, it can involve days or an entire week away and that might be seen as disruptive. Since speaking engagements are often planned months or even years in advance, you might have been very enthused about that topic, that speech, even that trip, when you first accepted, but with the passage of time, things have changed and your enthusiasm has waned.

But you are a professional speaker or even if you do not see yourself as a professional speaker, you should act like one. That means you speak, even if you don't feel like it, and you do the best job possible. The motto of "the show must go on" that actors and actresses live by is applicable for the speaker: "The speaker must speak."

Situation #12: Staying fresh when you give the same speech again and again to different audiences

Cavett Roberts, who founded the National Speakers Association, used to say that it's easier to change audiences than it is to change your speech. That's a powerful concept and one that is very reassuring to those who wonder if they should have several versions of speeches that they are giving. It can actually be the way to building a very lucrative speaking career if you have one speech that you "take on the road." Now the road may not even mean literally on the road to another location. It can mean, that you offer the same or a similar speech to other departments within your company. But the principle is the same: how can you take the same basic speech and freshen it up so it does not sound stale? Here are some tips to accomplish that:

1. Insert new or different examples, taken from the headlines or from your own research, so the principles behind your talk are the same but the facts and anecdotes to reinforce it are not.

2. Use audience participation techniques to get your audience involved in sharing about specific issues that you raise in your speech so their fresh ideas enliven your talk.

3. If you have given a similar speech over time, discuss what is the same or different in either your speech, you, your audience, the society you live in that distinguishes those two experiences and what life or corporate lessons can be learned by those comparisons.

4. As long as your delivery is varied, and you avoid retelling such a "signature" story that it has become just too familiar, covering similar but not the exact same points will not bore your new audience. Remember that it is a new audience even though your material is similar.

Note: If you are giving the same speech to the SAME audience, you'd better find that out and, if possible, develop NEW material so you do not have even one member of that audience feeling like it's "same old, same old."

Chapter 11
SPEAKING FOR AUTHORS

A colleague of mine who runs a speakers bureau once told me that she had been asked to engage a particular internationally renowned bestselling novelist to speak for twenty minutes during a group's luncheon. They were offering a fee of $40,000 plus all expenses to get him to the luncheon from his home. His answer? A resounding "No!" This author hated to speak. The speaker agent was stunned that anyone would turn down $40,000 for twenty minutes of his time. This author, who did not need the money, knew what he liked and disliked doing, whether or not he was a "good" speaker, and he had the financial independence to say "no."

By contrast, over a decade ago, I was asked to speak on a panel of authors at a regional library conference. Although I had been speaking professionally for many decades in addition to my writing career, there were others on the panel who were not proficient speakers. There was one particular author who was so nervous and stressed out by the speaking opportunity that he read from his book; he did not even read in a way that did justice to his writing. Although it was an unpaid speaking engagement for all of us, whether you're asked to speak for free or for a $40,000 fee, you have to be good at it or it may hurt your writing career and, even if it does not negatively impact on your book sales or your reputation as a writer, it could hurt your self-esteem.

Of course that particular writer could have said "no" when the library conference committee contacted him to speak on that panel at their conference. But almost all writers, and certainly most book publisher publicity departments and even freelance book publicists or literary agents, feel they need to say "yes" to speaking opportunities, as a way of generating book sales or as a way to build their "platform" as an author.

However, if you do a poor job when you are at the front of that room, whether you are on a panel and speaking for ten minutes, or you are the keynote speaker for forty-five, it can actually backfire in your goal of your speaking opportunities benefiting your writing career.

You might, of course, be someone for whom speaking "comes naturally" even though you primarily define yourself as a writer rather than a speaker. Bravo for you! You may still find this chapter helpful, but it will be optional for you.

If, by contrast, speaking is something you have to work at, the good news is that, for most writers, putting more effort into your speaking efforts will probably lead to increased comfort in front of audience, better speeches, and, from those more positive experiences for your audience, increased book sales.

I know it might not make sense that someone's speaking ability could motivate an audience to buy his or her book, or seek out his or her blog or published articles. But that's the association that most in the audience will make. "If so-and-so is this good a speaker, his/her writing must be amazing!"

So if you're going to speak, even if you're primarily a writer, put some energy into become a good and even an excellent speaker. If you don't want to improve your speaking skills, and if you don't want to figure out how to craft your speech in a way that you "seed" your speech so that your audience is much more likely to buy your book, or seek out your writing, that's fine. Just stick to the knitting, as they say (stick to your writing and stay away from the platform!).

But before you decide to do that and put down this chapter, let's look at all the amazing reasons you *should* become a good or great speaker as a way of enhancing your writing career.

How speaking can benefit authors

Here are the top reasons for putting the time and energy into speaking if you are a book author or any other kind of writer:

1. Especially for full-time writers who do not have other jobs that get them out in the world in a consistent way, speaking forces you out from behind your computer or laptop and to come in contact with anywhere from one to hundreds or even thousands of other people.

2. Preparing for a speech can lead to the research that becomes a published book. As mentioned earlier, that's what happened with my first book, *The Vegetable Passion: A History of the Vegetarian State of Mind*, published by Scribner's when I was twenty-six years old. It began as a speech for my public speaking class as a senior in college. I continued to research after college, through graduate school, and my jobs in publishing. I sent myself around the world, to India and Europe to do research for the book, and when I could not get a publisher, I went to The New School and asked if I could teach a course based on my research. Before I even taught the first class, I received a letter from an editor at Scriber's who had seen my course written up in The New School bulletin. She asked if I had ever thought of writing a book on the subject of my course. Of course, I quickly replied, "Yes." She asked me to write a book proposal. I was able to write a 100-page proposal off the top of my head because I was so familiar with the material after so many years of research. She bought it quickly and two years later the book was published, the first of more than thirty books that have been published over the next three decades, translated into thirty-two languages.

3. If you are researching a topic, you may be able to get valuable insights into that topic by polling those in your audience (with their permission, of course). You could distribute a survey to your attendees.

4. Speaking for a fee is a source of additional income to what you earn as a writer.

5. If you are allowed to sell books when you speak, it could be a source of sales. As I noted earlier, when I delivered the

keynote address on friendship at a *Friendshifts®* luncheon that an association in New Jersey created just for me, I sold ninety-eight books right then and there. Of course you may sell thousands of books online or through your publisher, or through self-publishing, through wholesalers, but you rarely get to meet those who are buying your book unless you speak.

6. If you do a bookstore author event, you may get more attendees if it's known that you're offering a "content rich" speech and not just doing a signing.

7. Speaking is a way to grow your fan base.

8. You can organize your research and thoughts on a topic by preparing a speech.

9. You can decide you do not want to pursue a book-length project because doing the research for the speech was enough for you.

10. You get to know a whole new group of people besides writers: speakers, speaker bureau booking agents, meeting planners, human resource managers, executives, various levels of employees at companies, and association leaders.

11. If you are asked to speak in other states or countries, you can get paid trips to faraway places that you've only dreamed about getting to on your own.

12. If you're looking for a reason not to have to write, or a distraction from whatever writing you are working on, preparing for and delivering, a speech is a great one.

13. You may get an adrenalin rush before, during, or after you speak that is exhilarating and very different from the way you feel before, during, or after you write.

14. Writing projects, especially books, are such long and drawn out projects that it's hard to say, "I accomplished this today." By speaking, you have accomplished something specific and clear: delivering a speech.

15. You learn from your audience. You can even get the idea for a new book from audience feedback. That's what happened to me when I was speaking at the bookstore at Northwestern University about my first popular book on friendship, *Friendshifts: The Power of Friendship and How it Shapes Our Lives.* An older man who appeared to be in his 70s, came up to me after my presentation and told me, in a hushed voice, that he was embarrassed that he had a friendship that ended. From his reaction, and from other audiences when I spoke about friendship, I realized that even though my book *Friendshifts* had a chapter or two on coping with friendships that are failing or ending, there was a need for an entire book to address that issue. A few years later, my next book on friendship, *When Friendship Hurts,* was published by Simon & Schuster (in the U.S.) and Better Yourself Books (in India), among more than twenty-five other foreign languages and editions of that book. So that one man who took the time to share with me after my speech set in motion the research and eventually the book that addressed an issue and a need that his comment had highlighted

16. Helps you to be more confident in other speaking situations, such as being interviewed on a TV or cable show, on radio, in person or over the phone with print interviews (for newspapers, magazines, or online publications).

17. It's nice to be asked.

18. It's even nicer to be asked back.

The drawbacks of speaking if you are an author

Speaking is an art and a craft distinct from writing. Both use words but the differences that occur when the written words becomes a spoken one are very real. Here are some of the drawbacks to an author if you decide to give one speech, or even to become a part-time or full-time speaker, in addition to your writing career. None of these drawbacks are insurmountable; you should be aware of each one so you are not caught off guard if one, more, or all of these situations occur.

1. The first obvious distinction is that you can edit your written words, not releasing those words to the public until you are absolutely satisfied, whether that means one draft and a few hours or scores of drafts and years.

2. Unless you are delivering a written speech that you have memorized — usually not the best way to assure a presentation that seems fresh, spontaneous, and engaging, unless you are a terrific actor or actress who can deliver lines effectively each time — you have to get it right when you speak without the chance to edit and correct.

3. Until you become comfortable speaking in front of an audience, nervousness may cause you to blurt out things that you never thought you'd say, in public! That's why it's so important to practice, practice, practice so you are able to be in control when you speak.

4. If you're in the middle of a project, and you know how hard it is to get to the point where you're "in the zone" with your work, speaking engagements cannot be changed. The project has to be set aside, whether for hours, if a nearby speaking engagement, or literally days or a week, if far away, such as when I went to Japan to speak and gave six separate and unique presentations in two days with the trip lasting almost a week. That takes into account the time getting there, the day before to recover from the time difference, and the day you lose when you fly back.

5. Your appearance is under scrutiny and if you're not comfortable with that or you've had a weight gain or loss that you're still adjusting to, that can be hard on someone.

6. If you are shy or reclusive, speaking in public can be a chance to break out of your shell or it can be an experience that is pure terror.

7. Public speaking helps you to learn to "think on your feet" but it can be a brutal learning curve till you've mastered it.

8. Criticism or critiques of your speech, including your presentation skills, are right there, in your face, unlike the reviews you can read in private, if you choose to read them at all.

9. Since every audience is different, you will usually be tailoring your presentation to that audience, unlike writing that one book that is then read by contrasting audiences but the book rarely changes.

10. You may put a lot of time and effort into a speech only to have it cancelled because of the weather or not enough attendees. Then what do you do with that speech especially if you were not paid for your efforts? Could you have spent your time working on that book that's due or those articles that need to be revised?

11. If you're sick, or your car breaks down, you have to somehow get there, or get someone there in your place, because one, twenty, nine-hundred, or several thousand people are waiting for you.

How to transform yourself from a writer to a speaker

How do you become a writer? By writing. You become a published writer by getting published. In the same way, you become a speaker by speaking. You become a public speaker by speaking in public. Unlike the solitary act of writing, you need an audience to be a public speaker. But, like the writer who needs to write, and keep writing, to improve his/her writing, you need to speak and keep speaking, before lots of audiences, to get the practice at speaking that will help you to improve your speaking skills.

In order to improve my own speaking skills, I read books about speaking. That's another way to improve your speaking that is available to everyone; in the References in the back of this book are just a few of the many books about speaking. Other books provide a reprinting of some of the greatest speeches ever given that have changed the world, such as Mahatma Gandhi's February 4, 1916 speech given at Benares Hindu University in India, "There is no salvation for India," which shared publicly his belief that India needed to return to its own identity following years of British rule, excerpted in *Speeches that Changed the World;* or the "I have a dream" speech, "Speech at the Great March on Detroit," June 23, 1963, by Martin Luther King, Jr., which so eloquently demonstrates the value of repeating a phrase — excerpted in *Greatest Speeches of Historic Black Leaders, Volume 1,* revised and updated, by Ben Anagwonye.

Besides reading great speeches, another way to become a better speaker is to attend conferences where you will see excellent speakers presenting. With that idea in mind, in 1996, I joined the National Speakers Association (NSA), an association founded in 1973 that has grown to several thousand members who are professional speakers; the association has more than 40 chapters. The annual national conference, which is held in a different location throughout the U.S. each year, provides an excellent opportunity to see top quality speakers in action since the crème de la crème are asked to present keynotes at the three-day conference usually held in July. I also joined a local chapter of NSA which offered an opportunity to attend monthly meetings with addresses delivered by visiting top speakers. At one of my very first chapter meetings I was offered an opportunity, along with the other attendees, to present a mini-speech. From time to time, I have been asked to present at one of the speaker universities that are organized; that is a way of showcasing my speaker skills to my peers.

There are numerous speaker associations headquartered in major cities around the world that are listed in the resources section in the back of this book that provide similar opportunities for their members and other attendees. Not only are you able to be exposed to great speakers when you attend their annual conferences, but you can learn about all the various topics and issues that speakers cope with, such as how to get booked or how to consider any cultural trends when you are speaking internationally.

There is also an international association that is dedicated to giving aspiring and beginning speakers a weekly opportunity to hone their craft by speaking in public. That association is called Toastmasters International. With local chapters throughout the United States and other countries— there are twelve different weekly Toastmasters International meetings in just New Delhi, India — there are weekly speaking opportunities offered where you can work on your presentation skills and you can also network with others who share your goal of improving their speaking skills.

In addition to joining associations, you can go to public events that are offered by world-renowned speakers. There is a phenomenon that has sprung up in the last few years known as the "TED" Talks (http://www.ted.com/talks). These are twenty-minute talks by some of the world's greatest minds; of course some are great speakers, as well as superb minds, and some are not the best presenters. But usually they are excellent presenters and that's why they have chosen to give a TED talk. You can find out what TED talks are being offered, and attend. You can also see TED talks at the website and you can see lots of speakers presenting at www.youtube.com

Speaking about your nonfiction book versus preparing a topic-based speech

If you are a book author, you are likely to be asked to give one or two basic types of speeches. The first is a talk based on the key findings of your book. The second is a talk that is "topic based," building on one of the chapters or topics in your book.

There are benefits and drawbacks to both kinds of speeches. The obvious benefit of creating a speech that focuses on your book is that you have already done the research so it is much easier to prepare a talk that highlights your book. There is the hope that by focusing on your book, your speech will be more likely to inspire sales.

For nonfiction authors, the drawback of giving a talk that summarizes your book is that you may say so much related to your book that listeners feel they no longer have a need to buy it.

A topic-based speech, even if it's related to your book but on a topic that was not covered in the book, will require additional research and effort to create a new speech. If possible, try to pick a topic that might lead to a published article, if you write out your speech. Pick a topic that you might add to the book, in an updated edition, or it could even become the basis of a new book.

If you do speak on a topic that is included in your book, make sure you have an organized speech or, whether right or wrong, your audience may assume that your book is a disorganized mess.

If your speech is topic based, you do not have to stick to your book exactly. If your book was published last year, and you find an amazing statistic in the newspaper the morning of your speech, you can certainly include that statistic in the opening to your talk. It's okay that it's from today and not from the one or two years ago when you were probably researching the material that became your published book.

If possible, if you have a choice of topic that you can speak on from your book, pick the topic about which you are most passionate and knowledgeable. Once again, there will be the assumption, whether right or wrong, that if you're this good with this topic, then the entire book is probably equally compelling.

Whether you are giving a speech that is an overview of your entire book or it is just one topic from your book, try to include in your presentation at least one or two sentences or even a paragraph or two from your book at a place in your talk that is a natural outgrowth of your speech.

This might seem like a manipulative way to expose those who have come to hear you speak to what you are as a writer, but that's okay! It is a way to encourage your attendees to want to read your book by letting them hear you reading from your book and that is a use of your speaking opportunity that makes a lot of sense. If you're a writer who speaks rather than a speaker who writes —and most writers are writers who speak — what better way to come to know you and your book than to hear you speak your words, the exact words, from your book?

Of course you should choose the words that you will quote from your book as part of your presentation *very* wisely. Make it the best words and the most provocative. Make it the ideas and actual words that would lead someone in the audience to say, "Wow, what wonderful words! I wish I could write like that! What a way with words!"

And when you're reading a passage from your book to the audience, do it with flair. And actually read from the book even if you've got it memorized and you're just holding the book — taking a moment or two now and then to look up and make eye contact with your audience — because that's the easiest and clearest way to show that it is indeed your actual book that you're reading!

Special concerns for the fiction author

Most nonfiction is topic-related so you are trying to get the audience excited about your topic, and impressed with your knowledge of the topic so they will want to buy your book for more information. By contrast, for the published fiction author, their work rises and falls on the author's style as well as the characters, plot, and setting for the novel, short stories, or children's books. The most effective speeches I've given, or heard, by fiction authors include both a discussion about how the novel or children's book came about, something about the novelist's or children's book author's background that is interesting to know and may not be readily known in the author's bio, *plus* reading from the work. It might be no more than a couple of paragraphs or one page from the actual novel to give a flavor for the writing, or reading a couple of pages, and showing the art work, from a children's book.

For fiction authors, you have that choice of whether you want to focus completely on your published book by reading just a short favorite passage or if you would also like to spend some or all of the time addressing your writing process or your writing career.

If you go to BookExpo America, held annually in May or June, usually in New York City, and attended by all the major publishers as well as booksellers, librarians, authors, and members of the media, you can go to the author breakfasts and lunches where you will hear a range of fiction and nonfiction writers, and children's book authors, presenting. You will hear how the top published fiction authors deal with the challenge of presenting a book to an audience; their goal, as is usually the goal of most fiction authors who speak, is to inspire the audience to want to read their book.

There are also regional book trade shows, such as NEBA (New England Booksellers Association) and NAIBA, held annually in the fall, that also have author events that provide a place to showcase yourself and your works and also to hear and observe how other fiction authors are presenting.

In New York City, there is also the Center for Fiction, located in midtown near Madison Avenue, which has free or reasonably-priced events where well-known fiction authors, such as Joyce Carol Oates, make presentations about their fiction. Once again, this is a wonderful opportunity to experience how well-known published authors deal with the challenge of speaking about their book or books in public. Ask yourself at the end of any public presentation that you attend, "Do I want to buy the author's book?" Of course if you just care about getting an opportunity to present to a new group of potential readers or fans, and you do not care whether or not someone is actually motivated to buy your book, your goals for speaking in public may be different. As a novelist or children's book author, you may care more about getting your name out there and getting out from behind your isolated computer than you do about selling books. In that case, whether or not you inspire your audience to buy your book may be an irrelevant question for you.

Bookstore, library or other author events

Since there are so many of these specialized events offered daily, it can be difficult to get someone to commit the time and energy to these author speeches.

Tips for getting people to attend your book events

The question of "how do you get people to attend a bookstore or library event?" is the subject of entire books on book marketing! It's an important, key topic, but in this book, let me just provide a few suggestions:

- Use your social media platform or presence to announce any forthcoming events including www.twitter.com, www.Linkedin.com, www.facebook.com, or specialized groups that you are on.

- Seek out local "niche" organizers who might have mailing lists to whom they can send an e-mail "blast." I recently used this strategy with a PR client who was scheduled to speak on his book at a chain book store in Baltimore, Maryland. Through "word of mouth" and the help of the community relations organizer for the store, I found a business executive who sent out e-mail blasts to thousands of local residents who had asked to be on his list for information about events they might want to attend.

- Ask the bookstore or the library if they have a list of broadcast, print, or online media that are likely to report on the upcoming event or even cover it when it happens.

- Find out the e-mail address for the Calendar of Events editor at local, regional, or national print or online newspapers that might carry an announcement about the upcoming book event. Most of these Calendar of Events departments require a minimum of two weeks' notice about the event so keep that in mind when you're planning your PR efforts.

- If you have a website, post information about the upcoming events at your site.

- Hire a freelance publicist to help you to publicize your events.

- Find out about local schools and contact the head of the department who might tell teachers to invite their students to your book event if it's on a topic that applies to that class, such as a history course, or if it's fiction, contact the English department.

- Team up with other authors so you have a library or bookstore event that can draw on the multiple platforms for each one as well as gathering together attendees from a potentially larger fan base.

Being memorable as a speaker

Whether five, fifty, or two-hundred-fifty people show up for your author event, make each person feel good that he or she took the time to come to your event.

Make it worth the effort of everyone in that room whether the event is free or they had to pay a fee and whether you sell one book or two-hundred. As noted earlier, if you make it clear that you will offer a brief presentation, in addition to a signing, you may get more attendees. If potential attendees think it is just a signing, only those planning to buy will show up. (This is fine if you're a household name or a celebrity, but for authors still trying to build a fan base, more incentives may be needed.)

Fiction authors will be expected to read from their published work and that's fine. Adding a discussion about how the book came about or other interesting information related to the book including writing the book may also help the fans to feel that they got something that they could not have gotten by just reading the book.

Nonfiction authors should prepare a brief ten to fifteen minute talk related to their published book so it is more than just a reading and signing.

Having bookmarks as a promotional give away or a pen or pencil with your name on it, and/or the name of your latest book, is a gesture that may be welcome by your audience, whether they buy your book or not.

Bring handouts and distribute those handouts with complete information about the book. If someone does not buy a book right at that event, they may decide to buy at another time. A handout, especially if it has worthwhile content so it is more likely to be saved than tossed, may just be the helpful reminder someone needs to direct them to a purchase later on.

Chapter 12
GIVING TV/CABLE INTERVIEWS

Some of the principles you learned in this book can be applied when you are asked for an interview by the print (magazines or newspapers), broadcast (television, cable, or radio) or online (bloggers, online publications) media, such as knowing your topic, and being interesting and prepared. But some tips are quite different since the time you have for a live television interview may be, at the most, five minutes and you have to be careful when you are interviewed by a reporter, for forty-five minutes to an hour or longer, that you remember it is an interview and *not* a conversation.

But media interviews, like speaking in public, if handled well can grow your reputation and spread your own or your company's brand in a way that is unmatched by anything except possibly advertising, but the media is free.

How to behave on television[1]

Appearing on television is an experience as foreign to most writers as sitting in a quiet room researching and writing a book would seem to most interviewers or performers. If you are asked to be interviewed on a local, national, or network TV or cable show, these tips may help your experience be rewarding, rather than embarrassing.

---

[1] This is a revised version of an article I wrote that was published in *Writer's Digest* in September 1975.

Before the interview
Be thoroughly familiar with your subject matter.

This may seem like an obvious suggestion, but remember that an appearance may be scheduled months or even years after an article or book was researched and completed. Reread your notes, your relevant published works, and recent publications by others on the same topic that might be discussed with you. You should be so well-versed in your subject matter that note cards are unnecessary. Memorize statistics, humorous or pertinent anecdotes or quotes, and exact citations that substantiate your major points. Because you are appearing before a camera, it will be unwise (if not impossible) to refer to even the smallest index card or scrap of paper.

On the average television show, you may be allotted anywhere from two to ten minutes for the interview, depending on the format of the show and its style. The format of the show may vary — e.g., you may be one of several guests, or you may be the only guest, but appear on just *one* segment of a longer show — but the typical interview usually boils down to about seven to ten minutes. Therefore, it is imperative that you have confidence that your answers are correct and that your knowledge of the subject or your expertise cannot be shaken by the barrage of questions that you may be asked.

Prepare a list of sample or recommended questions

Best-selling nonfiction writer Joseph Goulden (*The Superlawyers*) offered this piece of excellent advice to me. Some stations may be insulted if you provide them with a list of questions, but often an interviewer will ask you what you want to be queried on. The reasons may range from respecting the insight of the author into the relevance of his or her material, to the interviewer's hectic schedule not allowing him or her a chance to read your material. Regardless of the reason, it is desirable to prepare a good list of sample or suggested questions. Photocopy the list and carry it with you just in case you need it. (Of course it is a mistake to become conditioned to only those questions so that you will be startled if a host or hostess deviates from your list. You still need to be able to answer anything and everything that is asked of you in an informative and knowledgeable way.)

Some producers may also share with you a list of questions that he or she has asked the host or hostess to use. Once again, this list is only a suggestion. Some hosts use those questions faithfully; others completely disregard the list and ask different questions. Once again, be prepared to answer whatever questions the host or hostess asks, whether from your list, the producer's list, or that are completely new to you.

Set up practice interview sessions and/or, if necessary, get professional media training

For many authors, the initial talk show pre-interview, which is usually conducted over the phone in advance of booking you on the show, may be a definitive test that determines whether or not a subsequent TV or cable appearance will come to pass. Being excessively wordy on the phone or making the mistake of thinking you're having a social conversation with the producer or booker, rather than being pre-screened as a potential guest, could end your chance with a particular producer or show.

To give yourself the best chance at being selected to appear on a show, as well as to improve the likelihood that your actual interview will be all it could be, set up practice interview sessions. If you have the budget for it, hire a professional media trainer. Work with him or her to fine tune your TV presentation skills including what you will say and how you will say it. Ask the media trainer to videotape your mock interview. Play it back and discuss together what works and what does not work, and how you can improve, including your wardrobe, make-up, hair, and facial expressions as well as what you say.

If you do not have the budget for a professional media trainer, at least do a "mock talk show" session in your living room with a family member or friend conducting the interviewing. You can even use a home video camera to tape the session, as much for the feedback you can get when you review the tape as for the semblance of an actual interview whereby you are asked to avoid talking to the camera but instead asked to speak to the interviewer. Give your list of questions to a friend or relative and answer them as if you are on the air. Time your answers and see if you are taking too long to make your point. Try a second run-through with the interviewer "ad libbing" the questions. Just hearing your replies will be a learning experience since few writers, except poets and those who lecture widely, have a great deal of experience with structured public exchanges. You might even consider having a small audience at a practice session to familiarize yourself with an audience watching you while you are being interviewed.

Unless you're one of those rare TV "naturals" who thrive in front of the camera, without enough preparation, the hordes of persons at a talk show — camera operators, producers, engineers, other guests — may be disconcerting to someone used to only one other person being present during an interview. Ask the guests in the audience at the practice interview to comment on your answers as well as on your television manner. Do you seem relaxed? Were there any physical, especially facial, mannerisms that seemed annoying or distracting? Was your voice clear? Would your statements stimulate someone to want to buy your book? What's the one idea that someone heard that was especially fresh, memorable, or unique? Work on expressing yourself in a way that leaves a lasting favorable impression.

Select attractive and comfortable clothing

Most shows will advise you not to wear white (unless you're best-selling author Tom Wolfe who always wears his trademark white suit) or checkered garments, but after that you are on your own. Choose something that you have worn before and have received compliments on. (Or if you've gained or lost weight and have nothing that fits in your closet, go out and buy something new, even if you only wear it this one time and then donate it to charity afterwards because you *are* going to lose those 20 pounds you recently gained!)

If you wear a dark suit, you can always brighten it up with accessories, such as a scarf for a woman or a brightly colored tie for a man.

Of course, if possible, it is best to avoid buying something the night before your debut but sometimes it is not practical to avoid doing just that.

Whether your outfit or suit is old or new, pick clothing that fits the time and format of the television show — keeping in mind that many shows are taped and that you may tape at noon for a late-night program.

If you are told that you need not worry about what you wear below the waist because the camera will only be focusing on your face, remember that some shows do ask to have the camera pull back at the end for a long shot. Furthermore, even if no one sees your entire outfit, how you feel about how you look may impact your behavior during the interview. So I suggest you concern yourself with making choices that you are comfortable and pleased with including everything from your shoes to your overall outfit to what necklace you wear, if any, and even your watch and nails. The more confident you are about your appearance, the better.

Whenever possible, be familiar with the television show prior to your appearance

Of course everyone throughout the United States and even in many parts of the world is now able to see shows such as the *Today Show, Good Morning, America,* or *CBS This Morning,* as well as other national cable or network shows. It is harder to be familiar with the show you are going to be interviewed on if it is a local show, especially if it is in another city or state. If you know someone who lives there, you could ask him or her to tape the show for you and mail you a tape so you could preview it. If you're working with a book publicist, you could ask him or her to do that for you as part of his or her services. (Most book publicists network with publicists in other cities.) They may even know someone at the studio who would send out a sample show.

It is very important that authors who rarely watch TV, including

TV talk shows, gain a degree of familiarity with the way that talk shows generally unfold. This includes the pacing of the questions and answers, and the mannerisms that work and those that are annoying or counterproductive. So if you cannot preview the exact show you are going to be on in another city, at least try to watch another show that features author interviews.

Keep in close communication with the show's producer right up until your appearance

Stay in communication with the producer of your television show by e-mail or telephone prior to your appearance even if the interview was set up a week or two in advance. Make sure the producer or guest booker has your home, office, and cell phone numbers as well as your e-mail address. If you are going out of town for any length of time in advance of your appearance, make sure the producer knows how to reach you. A producer's biggest fear is a "no show" so make sure you are not contributing to that fear by being out of communication in the days or hours before your taped or live interview.

If you are traveling from out of town, arrive the day before the taping or live show. (Some shows require that you arrive the day before, even if you are taping in the afternoon and you could fly in that morning. It helps reduce the fear that there may be airport delays or other last-minute reasons that you are a "no show.") If you are in the same city the day before the show is taped or live, there is a higher probability that all will go smoothly with your appearance, or at least the part about getting there in the first place.

Remember that TV and cable are visual mediums

Some shows may actually ask you to provide products or visuals, besides just displaying your book jacket, so the show is more than just you and the interviewer asking and answering questions back and forth. However, if you do have visuals, you should mention if you are planning to display photographs or use props, since the director has to decide whether anything you wish to display is appropriate and, if it is, how it will be worked into the show. Television is a medium that incorporates the decisions of many diverse persons. If a producer decides illustrative material is desirable, try to be accommodating. However, ask for specifications as to the type of material that they prefer. Some shows use blow-ups of photographs or illustrations; others like slides; some will design the display material for the segment; others will request that you *not* show material.

Talking to the producer may also be helpful in clueing him or her into your goals for the interview. Often the producers write the questions for the interviewers and therefore they are the people most directly responsible for the actual vantage point of your interview. If there are other guests, you have the right to inquire as to their background so that you are prepared for any controversy or conflict that may develop. You might also want to consult their works, if they are published authors, so you might engage in a more knowledgeable discussion.

Try to have an expert apply your make-up

Some shows, mostly the network or major cable shows, offer professional make-up artists who provide a complimentary make-up transformation for their guests. For many local shows, or shows with a smaller budget, you will have to fend for yourself. Therefore, apply a light foundation to avoid shadows but do not try to imitate models or movie stars. Women should avoid harsh eye shadow or lengthy false eyelashes that may cause shadows. Light rouge is desirable, but too much of a "red" look will be accentuated by the color cameras. If you are doing your own make-up, the best advice is to use as little make-up as possible, rather than more than usual.

However, you might also want to hire your own make-up artist to give you as professional a look as possible. It may cost you anywhere from $50 to $250, depending upon whom you hire and her or his credentials and experience.

Arrive at the television station at the exact time you have been instructed — not too early and definitely not late

The producer will probably advise you to arrive at an exact time which will be anywhere from twenty minutes to an hour before your scheduled appearance (the longer time is for those shows where you will have a professional make-up artist working on you). Although you do not want to be late, you also want to avoid getting to the show too early. Producers are very busy and are often working on the questions for your segment and the rest of the show right up until the taping or live shoot begins. If you arrive too early, there may be no one to greet you or show you to the "green room" and your presence may be resented more than welcomed. If you arrive five to ten minutes before the exact time you were advised to arrive, no one will get that upset. But if you are coming a great distance and it's hard to judge how long it will take you to get to the studio, if you are more than fifteen minutes early, try to find a coffee shop nearby to sit and wait. At close to the time you were asked to arrive, now go to the studio.

Find a way to eliminate the tenseness you may be feeling

Kathryn Crosby, who hosted her own morning show on KPIX-TV in San Francisco, did simple calisthenics a few minutes before airtime to limber up and relax. Others find breathing exercises relieve the stress; others talk to the mirror or run in place. The technique is not important, but the result is — to soothe the body so that it responds to the television camera with ease and comfort. The key point is to eliminate the shaking knees and twitching eyebrow, for these will be magnified by the glaring electronic eye!

During the interview

All of the preceding guidelines were preparations *before* actual airtime. Those steps are necessary to avoid a disaster during the minutes of exposure. Now let's assume you are sitting in that red-and-blue checkered arm chair on the "So and So Morning Show." What are some technical tips about the interview itself?

Ignore the camera and the monitor

The most common mistake of the interview neophyte is to stare at the glaring, enormous television camera or the seemingly harmless monitor that is placed below the camera but tempts the guest because it replicates what is happening on stage. Unfortunately, if you stare at the monitor, you will be avoiding your host or hostess and the audience will not have the feeling that they are observing a casual conversation. You will appear nervous, uncomfortable, and threatened. Thus, at all costs, *look at your interviewer and ignore that huge, staring camera or that monitor.* Cameramen or camerawomen and others are paid to race around the studio "showing you" to the audience, so trust them to make sure that you will be seen and heard.

Keep your answers short, clear, and interesting

Remember this is a TV or cable interview — not a conversation in your living room with an old friend. You need to have short, crisp answers. Think in terms of "sound bytes." Express the information or anecdotes you want to share succinctly. TV and cable are fast-moving mediums. The worst thing you can say to a book author who was just interviewed on a show is, "Your answers were too long." (If it's a taped interview, that can be fixed. They will shorten your interviews for the aired version. If it's a live interview, you can't undo that and you may never be asked back.)

Somewhat related to the too-long answer is an even worse sin: being boring. If your answers are interesting, you may even be forgiven for taking too long to answer. But you will never be forgiven for being boring. Use your best material in this interview. (Hint: avoid giving your best ideas or information to someone you talk to in the "green room," the room you may sit in before you are brought into the studio for the interview. Save your good stuff for the actual interview. Or if you do talk to someone in the green room, or in the hallway on the way to your interview, and shared your best ideas and anecdotes, just say them again. The viewers have not heard them yet. It's new to them.)

Focus on connecting with the host or hostess, and your audience, and not on whether or not you are selling your book or yourself as a speaker

If you focus on your message, and on making a connection with the host or hostess, as well as your viewers, it is much more likely you will sell books than if you focus on selling your book. Phrases such as "In my book…" or "My book…" can be a real turnoff to your interviewers or the viewers. It is a definite art to convey information and anecdotes in a way that inspires viewers to want to buy and read your book. It could be that you share an example from your book that is so compelling that they want to find out more. Or the host or hostess expresses his or her excitement about your book for you. For example, an interviewer might say to you, "I read your book and it's excellent, by the way, and in your book you mention …."

Think of the interview like a job interview. If the interview goes well, you may be offered the job. If it does not go well, does it matter that you made a big deal about how many vacation days you were going to get or what the criteria are for end of the year bonuses?

Concern yourself with providing something to the interviewers and viewers that they need and they may want to find out more by buying your book.

If you're asked an annoying question, reply with taste and, if appropriate, humor

My sister Eileen, who has been studying and teaching communication skills, as well as practicing in the field professionally for thirty years, taught me early on an old adage to keep in mind when you're being interviewed: "You're not responsible for the questions, only for your answers." That means you have to find a way to deal with questions that are off the topic, or even offensive or annoying. You can of course state that you do not wish to answer that question, but it has to be done tactfully, and only in the most special of circumstances, or you may fail to appear the expert, knowledgeable author that you most certainly are and others expect you to be. (In professional media training, you learn how to use the concept of "bridging," whereby you respond to a question that may be off topic but you bridge it back to the ideas and information that you want to share.)

On a local show in Washington, D.C., Dr. Neil Solomon appeared in connection with his recently-published book on weight control. The interviewer, however, began her questioning with a completely unrelated question about why a certain type of packaging might be dangerous to children. I had tremendous respect for Dr. Solomon as he calmly and clearly answered her question; the hostess soon returned to weight and diet. Because Dr. Solomon was not "thrown" by a deviation from his book about diet, he won the respect of the audience and the admiration of the interviewer by *not* becoming hostile or disoriented. *Being flexible* is a key principle for a talk show interviewee. Otherwise you may seem forced, programmed, or out-of-control.

Some writers refer to their published writing, or the title of their book, in every other sentence. Rather than motivating the viewers to become readers, this often turns them off to the guest and his or her book. As noted earlier, if you are interesting, the viewer will be inspired to pursue your writing. There is no way to force television watchers to become readers through the repetition of a title or continually picking up your material for exhibit. If your comments and thoughts are provocative enough, there may be a residual effect to your discussions. *However, have your book on hand just in case they want to display it and they never received a copy or have misplaced the one that you or your publicist sent in advance.*

Of course you can engage in lively debates with an interviewer.

This is often preferable to simply being an overly-compliant guest who agrees with everything the host says because of the mistaken notion that to disagree would project the impression that he or she is impolite. But energetic conflict is different from emotional anger and wrath at a tactless or infuriating question. Try to engage the host in an animated but controlled discussion, but not by attacking or losing your temper.

"Time's up..."

When you are told the time is up, quickly end your sentence (if you were in the middle of a comment). But if you were not speaking, do not immediately begin talking as if you're trying to get in "the last word."

Some writers, unfamiliar with the split-second timing in television shows, cannot accept having to terminate a sentence when they had five more lines to say. This may have disastrous results. I remember my shock when I saw an author on *The Today Show* literally argue with Barbara Walters, who was the host at that time, after she advised him she was sorry their discussion had to end. "But I just wanted to say," a voice was heard echoing as the commercial instantly began.

Instead of getting flustered and confused when time runs out, smile politely and sit in your chair until the command is given to take off your mike. Often there are a few seconds when the camera moves back and covers the entire setting before going to a commercial break.

Try to allow a few minutes after the program for feedback and/or discussion

Producers and interviewers are usually very helpful to an author if the guest allows a few minutes to analyze what just occurred. If you very simply say to the producer or guest booker, "How do you think the interview went?" be prepared to hear some criticism and useful feedback as well as praise. If you get some helpful suggestions, such as

"You seemed a bit wooden at the beginning but you loosened up as the interview progressed," or "Your answers were too long," don't get defensive. Be gracious for the feedback and comments and let him or her know that you will be applying those suggestions in your next interviews.

Of course if your interview has been sandwiched-in among several guests, you may have to wait patiently in a special room until the show is completely over before discussing the show. But it may be time well spent. You may pick up tips on how to improve your television manner and you will also be able to probe any points that might have been made if you had just had more time. This shows your interest in the show and the people behind it and the exchange is beneficial for everyone. If you have another appearance right after the show that you have to dash off to, this is often a luxury, but sometimes there is at least ten minutes that you can spare to become more "television-wise."

However, if you are whisked out of the studio, and the building, of course don't be aggressive about asking for feedback. You can always send an e-mail or call later on to see if there are any comments that might be useful to you, be they positive or constructive criticism.

These points are just the basics for being a confident and desirable guest. Each televised interview you do helps you improve and master your talk show interview skills and manner. If you are appearing on several shows, do not carry the mistakes you make on one program to the next ones.

Learn from your errors, and approach each appearance with a fresh, enthusiastic attitude. Like Anthony Hopkins said, when he appeared in the Broadway hit *Equus*, you should make the viewer feel as if you have never said those quotes before, that *this* is the first time, and that they are the first ones to hear your "answers." Avoid sounding rehearsed, memorized, or planned. After all, a writer is even luckier than an actor in that you *are* composing a new script every minute for the questions will be varied and your answers will probably be equally diverse. Thinking you've "been there before" may lead not just to a dull interview but you might even embarrass yourself by answering the wrong questions with the right reply.

Try to make the time to write a personal thank-you note or e-mail to the producer, guest booker, and hosts. It may enhance their respect for you as a "people person" and also give them a feeling that they are appreciated for their efforts. This also creates a kind of meeting of two worlds — the visual and the written media — with the common goal of exposing ideas to the public.

To all the overall and specific advice about how to behave on television or cable, the best piece of additional advice I can conclude with is: "Enjoy yourself!" If you do, the viewers will share the experience and *want* to discover more about you and your ideas. Some may jump for the phone to order, rush to the local bookstore, or go directly online to get your book from an online bookstore. But even if they don't run out and buy your writing tomorrow, you — your name, your image, perhaps even the title of your book and, more importantly, what you said that's especially memorable and insightful — will be part of their collective memory and, hopefully, a stimulating part.

Chapter 13

IN CONCLUSION/SUMMING UP

H ere is my DYNAMIC approach to creating and delivering a great speech, whatever its length:

D =**D**ecide on your goal for this speech

Y =**Y**ou are the link between your audience and your information. You are the book, the play, the movie, the TV show. You are the way that they're getting the material — information, inspiration, interest — that they came to get.

N =**N**ever be dull.

A =**A**llay your fears by being prepared.

M =**M**aster your delivery through practice.

I =**I**nspire, Motivate, Inform, Educate, Entertain, or Persuade your audience.

C =**C**onsider your audience so that what you say is new and what they need to hear.

Whether you have to give a three-hour workshop, a five-minute eulogy, a one-hour keynote, or a forty-five-minute breakout session, you are in the enviable position of being able to influence the way people think, what they know, whether they laugh, and how they view a place, topic, or even a person.

Being a speaker is a privilege and an honor that should not be taken on lightly nor should it be dreaded or minimized. Yes, it is potentially more stressful because even if you get the concepts and the words "right," your audience keeps changing and what works for one audience may not work for the next one.

You can find that annoying and absolutely intimidating about your role as a speaker. Or you can find it exhilarating and challenging. The part of speaking that you will continually be surprised by and that as you learn how to "work a room" or "work an audience" in a more confident and successful way, you will be that much more comfortable in your speaker role.

I hope this book has helped you to learn more about this mysterious and oh-so-wonderful experience we call public speaking. If you get good at it, it will be helpful to you in every aspect of your professional and personal life. If you get great at it, the sky's the limit.

In conclusion, here are twenty tips for becoming an effective speaker. Some are restatements of points already made throughout the book, and some may be fresh and new. That repetition is okay. Any points that are restated here, I deemed worth repeating.

And, as you know from reading this book, using repetition in a speech, if it's done in a skillful and purposeful way, can be a very effective speaking tool.

Ditto for writing.

Twenty tips for being an effective speaker

Here are my best tips public speaking:

1. Do the necessary background research for each and every speech. Know your topic inside and out.

2. Write out a speech making sure you have covered every single point that is promised to attendees in the write-up about your speech.

3. Use the written version to create note cards either using PowerPoint or another note-taking method.

4. Practice your speech, timing it.

5. In a workshop or seminar setting, allow time for ice-breakers at the beginning of the speech as well as time for interacting with the audience, possibly using role playing or breaking up into small groups with one person presenting for the group, as well as five minutes for Q&A, and a conclusion.

6. Distribute and collect the evaluations after you conclude your speech.

7. Use the handout and possibly a promotional give-away as a reward for turning in the completed evaluation.

8. Whether you get thousands or hundreds of dollars for a speech, or you speak for free, put the same excellent effort into your preparation for the event.

9. If someone has to leave early, don't take it personally. He or she may have to catch a plane or a train, an emergency might have occurred, he or she might feel ill. Don't let it throw you and avoid in any way attacking any member of the audience. That is the fastest way to have the entire group turn on you since they will instinctively side with the audience member who is one of them against you, the outsider, the speaker.

10. Take an improvisation class. It can help loosen you up for feeling more comfortable in front of an audience.

11. If with practice and preparation you find you are NOT enjoying the speaking process any more than when you first started, it's okay to reevaluate if this is the right additional activity for you, besides writing. Remember best-selling superstar co-authors Jack Canfield and Mark Victor Hansen were speakers before they co-authored the *Chicken Soup for the Soul*® series. What career model will work best for you?

12. Not all speaking is equal. The demands and expectations of a forty-five-minute keynote are different than a one-hour workshop or a three-hour seminar. Try out all the different types of speaking experiences and see if there is a type of

speaking that you enjoy the most. If there is, consider specializing in that format.

13. Remember that it's hard to speak and write at the same time. Budget time before and after a speech as "down time" from your writing.

14. Respect and get to know those who ask you to speak and your audience but be careful about getting too friendly especially before your speaking engagement. You are the speaker, someone to be looked up to and revered. Walk the fine line of being accessible and concerned without reducing your prestige and authority.

15. Try to let it show through that you like yourself and your audience, and that you enjoy speaking. Even if you're tense or scared, avoid letting that show.

16. Arrive early to test the equipment (if the group is large enough that you need a microphone).

17. For speeches that require air travel, try to arrive a day in advance, just in case there are airport delays or cancellations.

18. If possible, don't leave your preparations to the last minute in case something comes up and you can't get to it. There's nothing worse than trying to "wing" a speech and having your audience disappointed that the presentation came up short.

19. Do your best and let go of the results.

20. Most people will feel an adrenalin rush before they give a speech. Instead of being afraid of those feelings, and letting it scare you or even shut you down, why not use it to your advantage so that you are energized and attentive when you speak.

Finally...

More and more speakers are being asked to send a promotional CD/DVD or online video to be considered for a speaking engagement.

The meeting planners want to see you speaking before an audience in an actual speaking engagement situation, not just you speaking into a video camera. I've been told that they want to gauge audience reaction as much as they are looking to see your skills as a speaker. Something to keep in mind since getting videos of speaking engagements is tough if you didn't plan for the videotaping at the time of the speaking event.

Remember at the end of Chapter 1 I asked you to make a video of yourself speaking? Now I'm going to ask you to take a few moments to do this exercise again. Prepare a five- to seven-minute presentation, complete with any audiovisual materials or props you might use, and set up your camera to videotape yourself, or ask a friend or colleague to take a video of you, speaking. You can use the same topic as the first time or switch to something else.

Once you have this second video, review it. Now look at the first video that you took. Compare the two. Do you see any changes in your speaking style? What about how you handle the topic?

Try to remember to take video of yourself speaking as often as possible and review that video, on your own or with another speaker or a speaker coach. If it's too hard for you to videotape yourself, record yourself speaking. (Most smart phones have a recorder built right into the phone.) You won't have the visual aspect of yourself speaking but at least you will hear yourself presenting. How quickly do you get to the core of your presentation? What's your energy level like? How loud is your voice? How articulate are you?

As you can see, being a public speaker means that you are continually working on yourself as a speaker. You work on the content of what you will be saying. You work on the delivery of that content. You even work on the audiovisual materials that will accompany any of your speeches as well as any written materials that you will be giving out before, during, or after your speeches. You work on your website so you update the video clips, or audio clips, that you share about yourself, and your speaker bio.

My very best wishes to you on your journey to more effective speaking. I look forward to hearing about your triumphs and, if it happens, your occasional disappointment. (And if all your speeches go well, bravo! Don't force a disappointment because you think that not every speech will be stellar.)

Thanks for reading this book and for being open to my ideas as I share my own experiences, and the research I've done on public speaking, from those first speeches I gave during my school years. Even now, I can remember those times when I had them in the palm of my hand. The audience and I were connecting and they "got" the points I was making. What a wonderful feeling that was.

I strive to make that happen in each speech that I deliver and I hope I have inspired you to make that connection happen with you and your audiences. By understanding some of the secrets behind excellent speaking, you can now apply these to your own speaking engagements.

Speak on!

Glossary

Agent Someone who gets a commission to find, and negotiate, speaking engagements for a speaker. Agents are usually attached to speaker bureaus and they get, on average, a 25% commission. It is usually difficult for beginning speakers to get represented by an agent. Agents have exclusive and non-exclusive representation. Exclusive means that they are the only ones associated with a particular speaker. Non-exclusive means that that speaker is represented by several agents or speaker bureaus.

Back-of-the-room sales This is when the speaker has one or more products to be sold before, or after, the speaking engagements. Products could range from a book, workbook, CD, or imprinted item (e.g., T-shirt or pen).

Bio Short for speaker biography. The write-up about the speaker that is put into the program, or that is used by the meeting planner or the person introducing the speaker to highlight the speaker's credentials and background.

Book To reserve a specific time and date for a speaking engagement.

Booking A confirmed date for a specific speech.

Breakout session A session, usually at a conference, when the larger group of attendees is broken out into smaller groups of twenty to one-hundred so that many speeches or workshops on a variety of topics are given at the same time.

Brochure Promotional piece often folded into thirds which describes the speaker and his or her credentials and topics; it could also be tied to a specific upcoming workshop that is being promoted.

Bureau See *speaker bureau.*

Cancellation fee Money that is charged by the venue if an event is cancelled, based on how many days before the event the cancellation takes place. (For the cancellation fee that refers to the speaker, see *Hold the Date fee.*) Cancellation fee can also refer to the portion of the registration fee for a public seminar that will be refunded to the attendee based on the amount of time from the event that the cancellation takes place. Cancellation fee policies and dates or number of days, should be made clear when you are contracting for a meeting space or accepting payment from a speaker engagement attendee.

Concurrent session See *breakout session.*

CSP Certified Speaking Professional. Distinction given by the National Speakers Association to those speakers who are members of the association and who have met a certain set of requirements to achieve this status.

CV Curriculum vitae. A detailed resume. A term usually used in academia for the biography of a professor.

Curriculum vitae. See *CV.*

Evaluation A review of the speaker's presentation requested at the end of the program, completed at that time, and turned in before the event is over, or requested later on and returned electronically, by fax, or through the mail.

Facilitator Someone trained to help a meeting along by asking questions, making sure no one monopolizes the available time, and handling the discussions and any key issues that the meeting planners or organizers want to have covered.

Flyer Descriptive promotional one-page sheet that covers the basics about an upcoming event, a product or an individual.

Gig Informal or slang way of referring to a speaking engagement or booking.

Global Speakers Federation A network of federation of speakers and speaker association from around the world that has an active website for posting about events and sharing information as well as a bi-annual conference that offers a two- to three-day program of educational and networking events at a different location around the world. Previous international meetings, known as summits, have been held in the Netherlands, South Africa and Singapore. The next summit is scheduled for Vancouver, Canada. Each year, there is a Global Speakers Federation meeting the day before the NSA (National Speakers Association) meeting begins.

Gross The total amount of money that is offered as a fee for a speaking engagement before any of the expenses or commissions to a speaker bureau are deducted.

Guarantee See *hold the date fee*

Handout An educational sheet, from one to twenty or more pages, that supplements the speech. A handout is usually distributed at the end of the speech but some speakers prefer to give it out in the beginning and for the attendees to use or refer to throughout the presentation.

Heckler Someone who boos or shouts out against the speaker.

Hold A tentative "hold" is put on a date before the "hold" is turned into a firm booking. See also *"hold the date" fee*.

Hold the date fee Professional speakers, or speaking bureaus, usually require a non-refundable percentage of the fee, usually 50%, to "hold the date" once the booking is agreed to. This fee might also be considered a "guarantee" for the speaking engagement; even if the association or company decides to cancel the event, the speaker and/or the bureau are entitled to keep this fee.

Honorarium A fee paid to a speaker that is usually a "token" amount rather than a full professional fee. It is a term and a tradition that is usually associated with academics or academia. When an executive or a professional speaker is asked to speak at a conference or event that is organized by a charity, or if their company does not allow acceptance of an honorarium, the honorarium may be donated instead to a charity on behalf of the speaker or the honorarium is turned down.

International speaker A professional speaker who speaks in countries other than his or her own.

Introduction The brief summary of a speaker's credits that is usually shared with the audience before the speaker begins his or her presentation. The introduction may also be published in the program for the event or conference.

Keynote A speech by one individual that is usually twenty to sixty minutes in length (with the typical keynote address forty-five minutes) that is considered the type of speech where a speaker can best showcase his or her expertise and speaking skills.

Keynote speaker A speaker who delivers keynotes or keynote addresses.

Lectern A piece of furniture that enables the speaker to get behind it and to stand in front of the audience. Also known as a podium, a lectern might be put on a stage so that the speaker is elevated above the audience enabling more of the audience to easily see the speaker. The microphone may be set up at the lectern although some speakers prefer a portable microphone or a mike that is attached to their lapel.

M.C. The Master of Ceremonies at a dinner or a conference or any event. This is the person who is charged with keeping the event moving along, calling on speakers or on those who will be introducing the various speakers.

Meeting Planner Someone who puts together the meeting, selecting speakers and handling all the various details from choosing the hotel or venue where the event will take place to what food will be served, if any, and what marketing or promotional efforts will be used to get an audience or, if an in-house corporate event, to make sure all the goals of the company are met. Depending upon the size of the meeting as well as the budget of the company, or, if it is a public seminar, on the budget of the organizers of the program, there may be multiple meeting planners involved.

Meeting Planners International See *MPI.*

Meeting site Where the meeting will take place. See *venue.*

Microphone An electronic device that helps someone to be heard at a meeting. A microphone may be part of the sound system at the event and be part of the lectern; or it can be a portable microphone that is supplied by the venue that is housing the event; or the speaker might have his or her own portable microphone that is brought to each engagement.

Mike Short-hand for microphone. See *microphone.*

Moderator The person who moves a panel along by calling on the various panel members to share their expertise or to answer questions that are posed.

Motivational Speaker A professional speaker whose primary function is to motivate the audience. Motivational speakers are especially in demand in any industry that relies on sales and selling for its success, such as real estate, automobiles, even the publishing industry, but there is also a need for motivational speakers in other service industries that have the potential for burnout because their jobs are so demanding such as social workers, teachers, counselors, and even students.

MPI Meeting Planners International. An international association of those who plan meetings as well as service providers to the meeting industry. Founded in 1972, there are more than 21,000 members with seventy-one clubs or chapters in more than eighty countries.

Net How much a speaker actually makes from a professional speaking gig by subtracting the amount withheld for commission. Usually expenses related to the speaking engagement, such as air fare, hotel, meals, and ground transportation, are paid for separately or reimbursed. But if those expenses are not covered by the meeting planner or company, those expenses would be deducted from the gross fee and that would also be a factor in what the actual net was for the event. If the speaker has promised to give away books or other products as part of their fee and they have to pay for those items out of their own pocket, those costs should also be deducted from the gross fee to determine the net income for a particular speaking engagement.

NSA National Speakers Association, an association of speakers started in 1971 which now has more than 3,000 members with thirty-nine chapters throughout the United States. It is also part of a network of speaking associations throughout the world known as the Global Speakers Federation.

Organizer The person who organizes a meeting. Also known as a meeting planner.

Panel When two or more people are asked to speak on the same topic at the same time in a meeting situation. There is usually someone who introduces the panelists and/or moderates the panel.

Panelist Someone who appears on a panel.

Platform This has multiple meanings. One meaning today is what is known as the "platform" for the book author or the speaker, meaning, how many people are aware of this individual? How big is their SOI (sphere of influence)? The word *platform* can also just mean someone who speaks from a platform, or the front of the room.

Podium See *lectern.*

PowerPoint A software manufactured by Microsoft that enables speakers to put their notes into a format that can be flashed on to a screen at the front of the room so that the entire room can see notes or video or photographs that are embedded in the PowerPoint. It is especially useful if someone is speaking to a room of thirty or more individuals whereby using handheld visuals, or using a flip chart, could not be seen by those toward the back of the room. Used effectively, PowerPoint can help a presentation. But, if your equipment fails, and you are totally reliant on your PowerPoint presentation, it can be a tough situation to overcome.

PR Public Relations.

Product What a speaker is associated with besides speaking such as a book, CD, or even imprinted items that he or she has created to reinforce their message or public persona.

Professional speaker Someone who gets paid for speaking and is considered a "pro" and not a "newbie" or an amateur.

Public relations Creating a public awareness of a person, product, or company.

Public seminar A workshop or seminar lasting anywhere from an hour to all day or even several days that is offered to the public rather than through an association or "in-house" by a company. Most public seminars are educational in nature with one or multiple experts delivering information to the attendees.

Q&A Question and Answer, the period at the end of a presentation when those in the audience, or even the moderator of a panel, are asked to contribute questions about anything that wasn't covered in the presentation.

Referral When someone recommends someone for a speaking opportunity or something related to speaking.

Repeat engagement When you are asked back by an association or company to do another speech, either on the same topic or on another topic but at another time.

Request for proposal. See *RFP*.

Retreat Usually a day-long event that is an intensive learning opportunity, gathering together those who share an interest, such as writers, cooks, or sales people, or put together by a company that enables some or all of the employees to learn and to network away from the headquarters or branch offices. Often speakers are brought in to educate or entertain those attending the retreat.
Return on investment. See *ROI*.

RFP Request for Proposal. When associations want speakers for their upcoming meetings, they will ask for an RFP, request for proposal, which potential speakers need to fill out by a certain deadline to be considered. Companies may also have an RFP, as well as the government, for a speaker to be considered for a specific speech or event.

ROI Return on Investment. In order to justify the time and expense of hiring a speaker, and having a program, companies as well as the attendees are asking to make sure that the speech or program that they attend has an ROI, return on investment. What did the time and energy spent in putting together, or attending, this event do to improve the company's bottom line? To help an individual to do something better or faster? Having an ROI that can be measured is the trend that meeting planners and companies are looking at rather than something vague like, "It was inspiring" or "It was interesting." Something more specific like, "A week after attending this session on time management I found that I was getting at least one more hour of productive time each day, time that I had previously wasted mindlessly surfing the Internet or allowing my co-workers to distract me."

Sell sheet A one-page sheet, usually in four colors, that sells someone's services or product.

Seminar A workshop that is usually more interactive than a keynote address that relies on one or many speakers to impart information and knowledge. The participants at a seminar expect to be asked to work on activities as part of the seminar or workshop with the speaker speaking only part of the time; the rest of the time, he or she is more of a facilitator, with the attendees at the seminar sharing from their own experiences and also learning by doing.

Shill Also known as a "plant," it is someone who is put in the audience to start the applause at the end of the speech — the idea is that if someone starts applauding, others will follow — or to ask a targeted question especially if during the Q&A no one else has any questions to ask. Needing a shill or relying on a shill is a practice that is not seen in a very positive light in the speaking business.

Signature story This is the story that defines a speaker. It is especially true for those who are motivational speakers and they begin their presentation by restating something dramatic that happened to them. It is considered rude and negative to retell someone else's signature story, especially without permission. Signature stories can make a speaker internationally renowned and famous if that story is powerful and memorable enough but it also has to be a speaking style used with caution because if you start to speak to the same audiences, those in the audience might see the story as repetitive or stale.

Social media A term that applies to websites, especially the well-known sites like Twitter.com, Facebook.com, and LinkedIn.com, that offer an opportunity to connect with others over the Internet for free or through a low-cost premium version.

Speaker Someone who speaks with the assumption that the speaker has put some thought, and maybe even some training, into his or her speaking skills.

Speaker bureau A company that handles multiple professional speakers, charging a commission for their services. The standard commission in the U.S. is 25% of the gross fee.

Speaker coach An expert at speaking who helps other speakers to improve their speaking skills. Speaking coaches may not be the highest paid speakers in the business, or even the most famous speakers, but they are good at explaining the speaking process and will work with their clients, in person, over the phone, or over the Internet, to review their speaking skills and to analyze how to improve what they do.

Sponsorship A company or individual who sponsors a speaker or an event by paying money for that sponsorship or just lending their name to help generate buzz and credibility by having that association.

Testimonial A recommendation, usually from the meeting planner, about a speaker's speaking ability based on their first-hand observation of the speaker in action. Testimonials may also be from someone who was in the audience, an attendee. The letter should be on official letterhead. If the testimonial is sent in an e-mail, as much contact information, including the person's title and e-mail, should be provided or at least available for any follow-up.

Topic The subject matter of a speech or presentation.

Trainer Someone who delivers a workshop relying on audience participation as well as lecturing as a way of delivering information.

Venue The physical location of a speaking engagement, meeting or conference, usually a hotel or a meeting center.

Video clip Footage of someone speaking, or appearing on television, which can be shared in its entirety or in a shortened sample format.

Workshop Also called a seminar, it is an opportunity for learning and training that ranges from a shorter version, forty-five minutes to an hour, to a half-day (three-hour), full-day, or longer format, with some workshops lasting five to seven days.

References

Alpert, Jonathan and Alia Bowman. *Be Fearless: Change your Life in 28 Days.* NY: Hachette Book Group, Inc., 2012.

Anagwonye, Ben, editor *Greatest Speeches of Historic Black Leaders.* Volume 1. (Martin Luther King, Jr., Barack Obama, Nelson Mandela, Jesse Jackson.) Benin City, Nigeria: Mindex Publishing Company Limited, revised and updated edition, 2010.

Barkas, Janet (a/k/a Jan Yager) *The Vegetable Passion: A History of the Vegetarian State of Mind.* NY: Scribner's, 1975.

Barkas, Janet. "How to Behave on Television." *Writer's Digest,* September 1975, pages 11-12, 13.

Booher, Diana. *Speak With Confidence.* NY: McGraw-Hill, 2002.

Canfield, Jack and Mark Victor Hansen. *Chicken Soup for the Soul.* Deerfield Beach, FL: HCI, 2001.

Canfield, Jack; Mark Victor Hansen, and Les Hewitt. *The Power of Focus.* Deerfield Beach, FL: HCI, 2000.

Dieken, Connie. *Talk Less, Say More.* NY: Wiley, 2009.

DiResta, Diane. *Knockout Presentations: How to Deliver Your Message with Power, Punch, and Pizzazz.* Worchester, MA: Chandler House, 1998.

Dormann, Henry O., editor. *The Speaker's Book of Quotations*. NY: Fawcett Columbine, 1987.

Fletcher, Leon. *How to Speak Like a Pro*. NY: Ballantine Books, 1983.

Frank, Milo O. *How to Get Your Point Across in 30 Seconds or Less*. NY: Pocket Books, 1986.

Goleman, Daniel. "Social Anxiety: New Focus Leads to Insights and Therapy," *The New York Times* on December 18, 1984.

Goulden, Joseph. *The Superlawyers*. NY: Dell, 1973.

Hartley, Mary. *Stress at Work*. London, UK: Sheldon Press, 2003.

Hayes, Derrick. *1 WORD Is All It Takes*. Columbus, GA: 2011.

Horn, Sam. *Take the Bully By the Horns*. NY: St. Martins, 2003.

Jeffers, Susan. *Feel the Fear and Do It Anyway*. NY: Ballantine Books, 1987.

Kador, John. Foreword by Lee Iacocca. *50 High-Impact Speeches and Remarks: Proven Words You Can Adapt for Any Business Occasion*. NY: McGraw-Hill, 2004.

Koegel, Timothy J. *The Exceptional Presenter*. Austin, TX: Greenleaf Book Group Press, 2007.

Levinson, Jay Conrad; RickFrishman, and Jill Lublin. *Guerilla Publicity*. Avon, MA: Adams Media, 2008.

Lontos, Pam and Andrea Brunais. Foreword by Rick Frishman. *I See Your Name Everywhere*. NY: Morgan James Publishing, 2008.

Montefiore, Simon Sebag (Introduction). *Speeches that Changed the World.* London: Quercus Publishing, 2007 (including 80-minute CD with 21 samples from speeches.)

Nierenberg, Gerard I. and Henry H. Calero. *How to Read a Person Like a Book.* NY: Simon & Schuster, Inc./Fireside, 1971.

Nilson, Carolyn. *Team Games for Trainers.* NY: McGraw-Hill, 1993.

Pausch, Randy and Jeffrey Zaslow. *The Last Lecture.* NY: Hyperion, 2008.

Preziosi, Robert C. *Icebreakers.* Alexandria, VA: ASTD, 1989, 2000. 16-page booklet.

Rand, Ayn. *Atlas Shrugged.* NY: Plume, reprint edition, 1999 (1957).

_____. *The Fountainhead.* NY: Plume, reprint edition, 1994 (1943).

Red and Black. (Tina W. Pennington and Mandy S. Williams) *What I Learned About Life When My Husband Got Fired!* Red & Black Books, L.L.C., 2009.

RIT (Rochester Institute of Technology). "Adult Learning." http://online.rit.edu/faculty/teaching_strategies/adult_learners.cfm

Schiffman, Muriel. *Self Therapy.* Berkeley, CA: Wingbow Press, distributed by Bookpeople, 1980.

Schultz, Chad. "Do people really fear public speaking more than death?" http://tmvision.org/speaking/people-fear-public-speaking-death/

Speaker. Magazine published ten times a year by the National Speakers Association. Included in membership dues or can be ordered by non-members through www.nsaspeaker.org. Offers excellent articles on all aspects of speaking, from the mechanics to tips on speaking skills to marketing and technology.

Stolovitch, Harold D. and Erica J. Keeps. *Telling Ain't Training.* Alexandria, VA: American Society of Training and Development (ASTD), 2002.

Thompson, George J. and Jerry B. Jenkins. *Verbal Judo: the Gentle Art of Persuasion.* NY: William Morrow, 1993.

Thomsett, Michael C. *A Treasure of Business Quotations.* NY: Ballantine Books, 1990.

Walters, Dottie with Lilly Walters. *Speak and Grow Rich.* Englewood Cliffs, NJ: Prentice Hall, 1989.

Woodall, Marian K. *Presentations that Get Results: 14 Reasons Yours May Not.* Lake Oswego, OR: Professional Business Communications, 1997.

Wydro, Kenneth. *Think On Your Feet: The Art of Thinking and Speaking Under Pressure.* Englewood Cliffs, NJ: Prentice-Hall, Inc., 1981.

Yager, Jan. *Effective Business and Nonfiction Writing.* Stamford, CT: Hannacroix Creek Books, Inc., 2nd edition, 2001.

_____. *Friendshifts: The Power of Friendship and How It Shapes Our Lives.* Stamford, CT: Hannacroix Creek Books, Inc., 1997; 2nd edition, 1999.

_____. *Grow Global*. Stamford, CT: Hannacroix Creek Books, Inc., 2012.

_____. *The Cantaloupe Cat*. Stamford, CT: Hannacroix Creek Books, Inc., 1999.

_____. *When Friendship Hurts: How to Deal with Friends Who Betray, Abandon, or Wound You*. NY: Simon & Schuster, Inc./Touchstone, 2002.

Resources[1]

Association for Speaker Training
Toastmasters International
Headquarters
P.O. Box 9052
Mission Viejo, CA 92690-9052
USA
http://www.toastmasters.org

At the website, put in your zip code at the "Find a Club" part of the site and you will get a listing of the closest Toastmasters clubs. Offers opportunities to speak in front of an audience and network with other speakers.

Associations for Speakers and Trainers

Speakers
APSS (Asia Professional Speakers – Singapore)
www.asiaspeakers.org
Founded in 2003

CAPS (Canadian Association of Professional Speakers)

---

[1] Disclaimer: Inclusion in this resource section does not imply an endorsement nor does exclusion imply a criticism of any services or companies that are omitted. Since contact information can change at any time, including website addresses, no guarantees can be made for the accuracy of any of the listings that follow.

www.canadianspeakers.org
Founded in 1997

FPSA (French Professional Speakers Association)
Founded in 2008

GSA (German Speakers Association)
Founded in 2005

MAPS (Malaysian Association of Professional Speakers)
www.maps.org.my
Founded in 2001

NSA National Speakers Association
http://www.nsaspeaker.org
Founded in 1973 — 39 chapters
An association of more than 3,000+ professional speakers who meet specific requirements to be admitted to the association. Local chapters offer opportunities to take speaking intensive training sessions and attend monthly meetings to gain knowledge of speaking skills as well as a better understanding of the business end of being a professional speaker. The annual meeting, held in July over several days, offers another opportunity to be exposed to some of the country's top speakers. If you don't attend the conference, you can buy the videotapes and/audiotapes/CDs of speakers and benefit from their presentations that way.

Note: Go to the website to learn more about each of these associations. Most have an annual or bi-annual conference, open to members as well as non-members, which provides an opportunity to see professional speakers in action as well as exchange information on the latest equipment or services for speakers and to network with speakers and experts.

NSAA (National Speakers Association of Australia)
http://www.nationalspeakers.com.au/

Founded in 1987

NSANZ (National Speakers Association of New Zealand)
http://www.nationalspeakers.org.nz/
Founded in 1994

PSA Holland (Professional Speakers Association Holland)
http://www.psaholland.org/
Founded in 2006

PSA UK (Professional Speaker Association United Kingdom)
http://www.professionalspeaking.biz/
Founded 1999
Current chapters in London, Midlands, North West, North East, East of England, Scotland and Ireland.

PSASA (Professional Speakers Association of South Africa)
Founded 2002
http://www.psasouthernafrica.co.za/

Trainers

ASTD (American Society for Training and Development)
www.astd.org
Offers extensive educational opportunities, in person through their annual and regional conferences, as well as through webinars and intensive workshops, with an emphasis on training and conducting workshops. Check their website for information on their upcoming meetings and trainings as well as what published materials are available that might be of interest such as papers on related topics like "ice-breakers."

SPEAKING COACHES

Note: Due to the miracle of www.skype.com and other ways of being connected across continents, it is possible to be coached online as well as over the phone and in person. Contact any of the coaches listed below to see if they are able to coach internationally or, conversely if they travel internationally so it is possible to meet in another country closer to where you live or in-between your two locations.

Max Dixon Communication
Seattle, Washington
www.Maxdixoncommunication.com
maxwdixon@gmail.com
Coaches on delivering more effective presentations.

Doug Stevenson
Colorado Springs, Colorado
www.storytelling-in-business.com
doug@storytelling-in-business.com
Stevenson focuses on how to use storytelling to make your point and to be a better speaker

Diane DiResta
31 E 32nd Street
Suite 300
New York, NY 10016
www.diresta.com
Author of *Knockout Presentations*, DiResta coaches on speaking skills.

Robert and Rande Gedaliah
www.SpeakingforResults.com
The Gedaliahs conduct a two-day intensive training session in New York City on how to speak several times a year. They also offer individual coaching.

Don Gabor
Conversation Arts Media

P.O. Box 715
Brooklyn, NY 11215
www.dongabor.com
In addition to networking and communication skills, Gabor specializes in how to organize and present a workshop.

Mike Landrum
www.coachmike.com
Landrum coaches speakers on everything from getting over stage fright and how to organize your thoughts into a speech to using PowerPoint more effectively.

Patricia Fletcher
www.patriciafletcher.com
A coach if you have an accent or dialect that you want to work on as well as if you need help with vocal production.

Vince Poscente
www.vinceposcente.com
Offers coaching on speaking especially delivering keynote addresses.

SPEECHWRITING SERVICES

Contact each service to find out about their fees and what they offer as well as how long they need to write a speech.

Inkwell Strategies, Inc.
www.inkwellstragies.com
Executive speechwriting.
You might find their free blog of interest:
http://inkwellstrategies.com/the-inkwell-blog/

EZ Speech Writers, Inc.
www.exspeechwriters.com

They write a range of speeches, from graduation, wedding, motivational, and executive, or they can take the speech you've written and for a fee improve it. Samples at their website.

Sheila Allee
http://www.sheilaallee.com/
Professional speechwriter with more than twenty years of experience. There is a blog about speaking at her website and she is also the author of the book, *Seven Steps to the Podium*.

MEDIA COACHES

Dunlap Media
New York City, NY
http://www.dunlopmedia.com
An award-winning broadcast journalist, in addition to his media training company, Steve Dunlap, founder and chief media specialist of Dunlap Media, works part-time in network news including CBS News.

Alan Stevens
London, UK
http://www.mediacoach.co.uk/
Works with individuals and companies on how to get their point across in the media including media coaching and crisis media management.

World News and Information Network, Inc.
www.worldnewsandinformationnetwork.com
See listing under Publicity Services for Speakers.

ONLINE DATABASES TO GET LISTED AS A SPEAKER

Speakermatch
www.Speakermatch.com

Paid subscription service which will send you possible speaker bookings based on the areas of expertise that you select. Then you write a proposal and pitch yourself to the individuals that are selecting from the various speakers. Includes free and ongoing speaker opportunities as well as paid opportunities.

Workplace Speaker Network
http://www.workplacespeakernetwork.com
Subscription service for speakers who especially speak on work-related topics. Based in Canada but open to speakers in any location.

Expert Click
http://www.expertclick.com/
Publisher of the annual *Yearbook of Experts, Authorities, and Spokespersons*. Speakers pay a fee to be listed at the website with a profile that is also included in the book which is available for free as a pdf file at the website to the media and meeting planners.

SPEAKER BUREAUS

Note: This is an option once you are at a level of professionalism that you are consistently speaking before paid audiences and getting excellent reviews for your speeches.

Traditionally, speaker bureaus get 25% of the fee that their speaker is getting. Their service is usually provided to those needing to find a specific client speaker or a speaker within a certain price range or category, such as a celebrity speaker or a bestselling author.

There are bureaus that handle speakers only on an exclusivity basis; others will allow you to be listed with multiple bureaus in a non-exclusive capacity.

Some bureaus only want speakers who generate a $5,000 and up fee and/or are celebrities in their particular field and their speaking fee is in the tens of thousands of dollars.

Go to the website for any of the speaker bureaus you are considering and see what their guidelines are for submitting your material for consideration. Most speaker bureaus require a video of you giving a recent paid speech as well as testimonials, a "bureau friendly" one-sheet, which means that it is full of contact information including your website, a recent photograph, testimonials from one or more recent meeting planners who saw you speak, as well as a list of topics that you speak on and a price sheet of fees for keynotes or workshops, whether locally or out of town.

Remember, if a speaker bureau lists you, you still have to help by driving interest to them or their site with requests for your services. Although some bureaus may have to include at least two more speakers if they are contacted for your services, so it shows that the association or company did due diligence in determining who would be the best speaker, but if you are singled out and put up against two other speakers you have better odds of getting selected than if you're up against the 1,000 or more speakers in their bureau.

International Association of Speaker Bureaus
http://www.iasbweb.org/
Membership association, founded in 1986, represents speaker bureaus in more than fifteen countries. There is an annual conference for education, skills development, and networking. In addition to presenting as part of the program, there are speaker showcase opportunities for speakers to be seen by the attending bureaus.

www.internationalspeakers.com

www.leadingauthorities.com

http://premierespeakers.com/

www.harrywalker.com

www.simonspeakers.com (Simon & Schuster, Inc. authors who are also speakers)

www.authorsunlimited.com

www.eaglestalent.com/speakers

http://www.businessspeakersbureau.com/

www.speakers.com
Started in 1994. Offers meeting planners two options: search on their own or use their search consultants for help.
To find out what you need to send in order to be considered as a speaker with this bureau, go to:
http://www.speakers.com/article.asp?id=8
(This is a good prototype of what most speaker bureaus will want you to send.)

PLACES TO LIST YOUR UPCOMING EVENTS

Event Brite
www.Eventbrite.com
A website and service that allows speakers to post information about an upcoming speaking event, even free ones. The site collects a fee only if you charge for admission and individuals sign up. Payment is handled through www.paypal.com.

PUBLICITY FOR SPEAKERS

Here are just a few publicity companies that offer a range of public relations services for speakers and experts. Fees and services differ with each company.

Pam Lontos Consulting
http://www.pamlontos.com/

Pam Lontos specializes in providing PR services to speakers. Since selling her company, she is now doing PR consulting. She is the author of the related book, *I See Your Name Everywhere*.

Jill Lublin
http://www.jilllublin.com/
Lublin, a professional speaker herself, offer PR consulting; she can also put together a full promotional campaign. She is the co-author of several bestselling books about PR including *Guerilla Publicity*, co-authored with Jay Conrad Levinson and Rick Frishman.

Darcie Rowan Public relations
darcie.rowan@verizon.net
Publicist in the New York City area who has a range of clients and offers various publicity packages including a blogger campaign.

Kim McMillon
http://artsinthevalley.wordpress.com
California-based publicist who also does a weekly Internet radio interview show with experts, speakers, and authors.

Promotion in Motion
www.promotioninmotion.net
California-based publicity firm started and run by Irwin Zucker getting publicity for speakers, authors, performers, and others.

World News and Information Network, Inc.
http://www.worldnewsandinformationnetwork.com
fyagerpr@gmail.com
The company that my husband Fred Yager and I run that offers publicity coaching or direct services for speakers who are looking to get more media exposure. At the website you will find a list of available services listed included writing a press release and creating a press kit, pitching to broadcast, print, and online media, media coaching, foreign rights coaching, ghostwriting, and more.

FREE ONLINE PUBLICITY SERVICES THAT JOURNALISTS AND THE MEDIA CAN USE TO FIND EXPERTS

Below are several free online services that you can subscribe to that have daily free listings of journalists looking for experts. Each service has its own distinctions and the media may be more likely to post in one service over the others. You can decide to subscribe to, and monitor, all three services or try them all for a while and see which one is best for your needs. You or your assistant would then follow-up with a pitch to any broadcast or print journalist that seems to be a good fit with your expertise. Occasionally there is a call for a speaker also posted but almost all of the postings are for possible publicity opportunities.

http://www.reporterconnection.com

http://www.helpareporterout.com (HARO)

http://www.pitchrate.com

APPENDIX

NEW SPEAKING ENGAGEMENT INQUIRY FORM

Name
Title
Company
Address
E-mail
Phone
Website

Source of the referral

Do you have a specific date in mind?

Type of speech? Keynote? Concurrent (break out) session?

Topic?

Length?

What is the occasion? Conference? Company-wide meeting?
In-house training? Association trade show? Other?

Who is the audience?

Estimated size of the audience

Budget?

Other details?

Next step:

CONFIDENTIAL PRE-SEMINAR SURVEY
"Speaking Secrets for Authors"
Your seminar leader Jan Yager, Ph.D.
New York City
(Please clearly print your answers)

NAME _____

ADDRESS _____

_____

(City, State, Zip Code)

E-MAIL _____

WEBSITE (if any) _____

Have you published any books? Yes | No

If yes, please list titles, publication date, and genre (e.g., nonfiction, fiction)

_____

If you have a job besides writer, what is it?

_____

What training have you had as a speaker?

_____

Do you belong to any speaker associations? Yes | No if yes, please list:

_____

What is your Number One goal for tonight's seminar:

_____

What is your goal as a speaker?

_____

What is your goal as a writer?

_____

Thank you for your time and answers!
Your seminar leader Jan Yager, Ph.D. (jyager@aol.com)
http://www.drjanyager.com

KEYNOTE PREPARATION WORK SHEET

Working title of this speech: _____

Date : _____

Practice session(s): _____

Keynote: Length _____

Audience: _____

Opening: _____

_____

_____

Point #1: _____

_____

_____

Point #2: _____

_____

_____

Point #3: _____

_____

_____

Closing: _____

_____

_____

Audio-visual materials: _____

_____

_____

_____

Handouts: _____

_____

_____

FEEDBACK/EVALUATION

Presentation by (NAME)

(FILL IN CONTACT INFORMATION)

Thank you, in advance, for taking the time to fill out this evaluation.

Presentation: _____ **Date:**_____

What is the one idea you learned during this presentation that you are going to use first?

_____

_____

Please let the presenter know what you liked most about this presentation:

_____

_____

May we have permission to use your above quote about this program?
Yes_____ No _____

Please rate this presentation: Excellent _____ Good _____ Poor _____
Other _____ (fill in)

Please provide your contact information for post-presentation follow-up.

(Note: Your contact information, including your e-mail address, will not be shared with anyone else.)

Name _____ E-Mail_____
Title: _____ Office Phone_____
Agency/Department/Company:_____
Address:_____
Fax:_____

(Note: You of course also have the option of turning your evaluation in anonymously.)

What other seminars might you attend in the future?

_____

Other topics? _____

Thank you for attending my presentation and for completing this feedback/evaluation form. I welcome your post-presentation communications.

Index

request for proposal See *RFP*
research, 20, 39-43, 103-104, 123-124
retreat, 163
return on investment, 163, 164
rewards, 16, 122-125
RFP, 163
roast, 88-89
Roberts, Cavett, 119
ROI See *return on investment*
Rotary Club, 1
running out of time to speak, 117
Russia, 9

S
seating arrangement, 15, 56, 94-95
secrets of terrific speakers, 3, 39-54, 155
    secret #1: It starts with your ideas, 39-40
    secret #2: After ideas, it's the articulation…40-42
    secret #3: focus on how you are going to say it, 42-43
    secret #4: know your audience, 43
    secret #5:prepare your own introduction, 44
    secret #6: be prepared, 44-46
    secret #7: share about yourself as much as you're comfortable doing, 46-47
    secret #8: get the audience involved, 47-48
    secret #9: don't let them know you're scared, 48-49
    secret #10: give the speech you want to hear, 49-51
    secret #11: learn from each speaking engagement what went right and what didn't, 51-53
    secret #12: develop your own speaking style and brand, 53-54
sell sheet, 164

seminar, 43, 58, 59, 163 *See also* workshop
    pre-seminar survey, 186
7 Habits of Highly Effective People (Covey), 40
Shankman, Peter, 16
shill, 164-165
signature story, 2, 120, 165
silence, 36-37
singing, 51, 52
Skype, 84, 85, 103
smart phone, 14, 16, 154
social media, 22, 66, 133 *See also* Facebook.com, LinkedIn.com, Twitter.com
Solomon, Dr. Neil, 146
someone walks out, 107, 152
Spain,
Speak and Grow Rich (Walters and Walters), 45-46
Speak With Confidence (Booher), 107
speaker agent See *agent*
speaker bureau, 88, 157, 165, 178-180
speaker coach, 165, 175-176
speaker evaluations, 72, 73, 152
speaker introduction,
speaker one-sheet,
Speakermatch.com, 177-178
speaking,
    5 "I"s of memorable speeches, 50-51
    arrival for, 153 *See also* punctuality
    expertise, 87
    fear of, 2, 3, 21-22, 102-107
    fee, 8, 152
    for authors, 28, 121-135
     keynote, 64-77
    last minute, 91-92, 116-117
    mechanics, 93-101
    no fee, 152
    preparation, 4, 12, 13, 27-29, 40-41, 44-45, 103-104

Williams, Mandy, 60-61
Winget, Larry, 9, 53
Wolfe, Tom, 139
workshop, 34, 56, 74, 77-83, 166
workshop (all day), 77-83
World News and Information
Network, Inc., 177, 181
writing, 5 *See also* authors as
speakers
writing for speakers, 4
writing out a speech, 4, 7, 40-42

Y
yawning, 110 *See also* booed
*Yearbook of Experts, Authorities,
and Spokespersons*, 178
youtube.com, 1, 10, 46, 66, 74,
76, 89, 129

Z
Zaslow, Jeffrey, 23-24

About the Author

DR. JAN YAGER is the author of thirty-two books translated into thirty-two languages. She speaks to corporate, association, and government audiences, as well as conducts public seminars, throughout the United States and internationally including in India, England, the Netherlands, and Japan, on a wide variety of topics such as:

- How to Speak in Public So They Ask You Back Again
- Work Less, Do More
- Write Your Way to the Top: Better Business Writing
- The Power of Friendship at Work & in Your Personal Life
- Grow Global
- Productive Relationships
- How to Meet the Love of Your Life

Her award-winning books include: *Business Protocol; Work Less, Do More; When Friendship Hurts; Friendshifts®; Productive Relationships; Career Opportunities in the Publishing Industry, 365 Daily Affirmations for Time Management; 365 Daily Affirmations for Happiness; 365 Daily Affirmations for Friendship; Road Signs on Life's Journey;* novels, *The Pretty One, Untimely Death* and *Just Your Everyday People* and a children's book series including *The Cantaloupe Cat* and the forthcoming *The Quiet Dog* and *The Reading Rabbit*, all illustrated by Mitzi Lyman.

For more information, go to: www.drjanyager.com
E-mail address: jyager [at] aol.com

Mailing address:
Dr. Jan Yager
1127 High Ridge Road, #110
Stamford, CT 06905-1203 USA

CPSIA information can be obtained at www.ICGtesting.com
Printed in the USA
LVOW101016230213

321379LV00002B/2/P